GW00543790
TORRES STRAIT
Thursday Island
Cape York
Jardine River National Park
Jardine River
Weipa
GULF
OF
CARPENTARIA
Groote Eylandt
CAPE YORK PENINSULA
Coen
Archer River
Cape Melville
Coral Sea
Endeavour River National Park
Cooktown
Normanby River
Mitchell River
Mornington Id
SOUTH PACIFIC OCEAN
Daintree
Cape Tribulation
Pt Douglas
Cairns
ATHERTON TABLELAND
Chillagoe
Mungana Caves National Park
Innisfail
GREAT BARRIER REEF
Burketown
Karumba
Normanton
Gilbert River
GULF COUNTRY
Croydon
Georgetown
Tully
Norman River
Ingham
Gunpowder
Camooweal
Leichhardt River
Flinders River
Townsville
Ayr
Rankin R.
Mount Isa
Charters Towers
Bowen
Proserpine
Hook Island
WHITSUNDAY GROUP
Richmond
Hughenden
QUEENSLAND
GREAT DIVIDING RANGE
Mackay
Collingwood
Winton
Georgina
Boulia
CHANNEL COUNTRY
Aramac
Clermont
Longreach
Thompson River
Barcaldine
Marlborough
Fitzroy R.
Emu Park
Emerald
Rockhampton
Bedourie
Diamantina River
Barcoo River
Comet R.
Gladstone
Carnarvon National Park
Biloela
Windoora
Lady Elliot Island
Tropic of Capricorn
Birdsville
Eyre Creek
Adavale
Bundaberg
Dawson Range
Maryborough
Fraser Island
Innamincka
Quilpie
Charleville
Roma
Gympie
Double Island Pt
Noosa
Dig Tree
Cooper Creek
Merty Merty
Nocundra Hotel
Thargomindah
DARLING DOWNS
Toowoomba
Brisbane R.
Moreton Island
Brisbane
STRZELECKI DESERT
Warrego
St George
Goondiwindi
Lamington National Park
Surfers Paradise–Gold Coast
Coolangatta – Tweed Heads
Murwillumbah
Cape Byron
Sturt National Park
Tibooburra
Dumaresq River
Texas
Gammon Ranges National Park
Lake Callabonna
Lyndhurst
Arkaroola
Lake Frome
Lightning Ridge
Moree
Tenterfield
Collarenebri
Glen Innes
Gibraltar Range National Park
Bourke
Walgett
Guy Fawkes River National Park
Grafton
FLINDERS RANGES
Wilpena
BARRIER RANGE
Paroo River
Namoi River
Narrabri
Armidale
Nymboida
NEW SOUTH WALES
Wilcannia
Silverton
Hawker
Cockburn
Broken Hill
Cobar
Tamworth
Hat Head National Park
Coonabarabran
Warrumbungle National Park
Port Macquarie
Crowdy Bay National Park
Yunta
Menindee
Darling River
Dubbo
Gulgong
Gloucester
Barrington Tops National Park
Burra
MT. LOFTY RANGES
Willandra National Park
Condobolin
Forbes
Mudgee
Hunter River
Mungo National Park
Hill End
Myall Lakes
BAROSSA & CLARE VALLEYS
YORK PENINSULA
Wentworth
Lachlan River
Orange
Bathurst
BLUE MTNS.
Gosford
Newcastle
Lord Howe Island
Gulf St. Vincent
Mildura
Murray
Hay
Griffith
Jenolan Caves
Lithgow
Hawkesbury River
Adelaide
Glenelg
Cove
FLEURIEU PENINSULA
Wyperfield National Park
Murrumbidgee
Wagga Wagga
Young
Berrima
Sydney
Swan Hill
RIVERINA
Goulburn
Encounter Bay
Goolwa
Victor Harbor
Lake Alexandrina
Hopetoun
Kerang
Tumut
Nowra
Jervis Bay
Tasman Sea
Kingston
Echuca
Chiltern
Albury
CANBERRA (ACT)
Murramarang National Park
Tallangatta
Horsham
Naracoorte
THE GRAMPIANS
Mt Buffalo National Park
Bright
Narooma
Kosciuszko National Park
Mt Hotham
Lind National Park
Mount Gambier
Melbourne
Yarra River
Snowy River
Eden
Alfred National Park
Portland
Port Phillip Bay
Mallacoota
Croajingolong National Park
Cape Bridgewater
OTWAY RANGE
Lorne
Lakes Entrance
Gippsland Lakes Coastal Park
Port Campbell
Cape Otway
Port Albert
VICTORIA
Wilsons Promontory National Park
King Island
Bass Strait
Flinders Island
Cape Grimm
Stanley
N
Bridport
Cradle Mountain Lake St Clair National Park
GREAT WESTERN TIERS
Deloraine
Beulah
Launceston
Queenstown
Evandale
Strahan
Gordon River
Derwent River
Apple Creek
Bicheno
Coles Bay
TASMANIA
New Norfolk
Freycinet National Park
Hobart
FORESTIER PENINSULA
Geeveston
TASMAN PENINSULA
Port Arthur
Southwest National Park
Dover

The Magic of AUSTRALIA

The Magic of AUSTRALIA

TEXT BY BRUCE ELDER
with contributions by Dalys Newman and Kathrine Bell
Photographs by Geoff Higgins and Ken Stepnell

Bluestone Press

Published by
Bluestone Press
Rear, 1 Hartnett Drive, PAK Logistics Building,
Seaford, Victoria, 3198, Australia
Phone: (03) 9776 4330 Fax: (03) 9776 4660
Mobile: 0413 795 460
email: gblackso@bigpond.net.au

Produced for the publisher by
Jentri Quality Books Pty Ltd
35 Borgnis Street, Davidson, New South Wales,
Australia, 2085
Publishing Director: Marion Child
Marketing Director: David Jenkins

Produced, edited and designed by Marion Child
Pre-press processing by James Young
Printed in Indonesia

First published 2002
Fully revised edition 2004

ISBN: 0-9752428-2-2

Page 1: The Twelve Apostles can be seen from the Great Ocean Road on the south coast of Victoria.
Page 2: Late afternoon sun on the Chase Range in the Flinders Ranges, South Australia.
Page 3: A reconstruction of a settler's home at the Pioneer Settlement, Swan Hill, Victoria.
Left: The 800 metre Murchison River has carved deep gorges and winding valleys out of the coastal sandstone of Kalbarri National Park in Western Australia.

Contents

Kangaroo Point, Hobart in 1888.

Top: Torres sighting Cape York.

Above: The Commonwealth Flag. Based on the Blue Ensign (a blue background with the Union Jack in the upper left hand quarter), the flag has the stars of the Southern Cross to the right. Below the Union Jack is a large, seven pointed star representing the Commonwealth of Australia (one point for each of the six states and one for the territories as a group). The flag was chosen in 1901 after a competition sponsored by the government.
The large star originally had six points , the seventh being added in 1908.

Above, right: The Duyfken in the Gulf of Carpentaria.

Right: Bass and Flinders in the Tom Thumb.

Centre: Captain James Cook. who first navigated the east coast of Australia

Far right: Australia's floral emblem Golden Wattle *(Acacia pycnantha)*

AUSTRALIA: The Heritage

by Bruce Elder (with contributions by Dalys Newman)

THE HISTORY OF AUSTRALIA is deceptively simple and uncomplicated. With no internal struggles and no serious external threats the country has evolved in a series of neatly defined periods of change.

The country's original inhabitants probably arrived about 50 000 years ago. These early residents, ancestors of modern-day Australian Aborigines, spread throughout the country over the next 30 000 years. They continued their uncomplicated lives, spending most of their waking hours engaged in hunting and gathering, until the late eighteenth century when Britain decided that Australia would make an ideal penal colony for many of the inmates of London's prisons.

The arrival of convicts at Port Jackson in 1788 was followed by a fifty-year period when settlements were established around the coastline and large tracts of fertile land were settled by sheep and cattle graziers.

By the 1840s the concept of Australia as a penal colony was being seriously questioned by liberals and reformers. The 'convict' period of Australian history came to an abrupt end with the discovery of gold. For the next thirty years miners from all over the world arrived in Australia. The goldfields in New South Wales, Victoria, Western Australia and Queensland yielded rich harvests.

The end of the nineteenth century saw the colonies, which had all become autonomous states, drawing together to create a unified federation: a country with a clear identity.

Australia in the twentieth century has slowly emerged from an unconfident ex-colony trying to assert its independence to a confident nation actively involved in the development and prosperity of its own region and committed to the broader international community through such agencies as the United Nations.

The search for identity has been unceasing. Throughout the century images of Australia have ranged from bronzed Anzacs to urbane city dwellers. The enduring images have always contained elements of sturdy independence, a refusal to respect authority, a genuine sense of egalitarianism, a dislike of pretentiousness and a sense of energy and exuberance. No matter whether Australians live in cities (as most people do) or work in the 'outback' these qualities endure. The result is a sense of identity which emphasises informality and independence. These qualities

Land ho!

seem so natural whenever anyone takes an overview of the country's development.

Aboriginal settlement before the arrival of Europeans

Modern understanding of early Aboriginal settlement is based on careful analysis of scarce, and often ambiguous, archaeological data. It is now accepted that the ancestors of modern Aborigines arrived on the continent at least 40 000 years ago. This is supported by evidence of camp sites in the south-eastern and south-western parts of the country which date from that period.

Some archaeologists believe that the first Aborigines arrived as early as 50–55 000 years ago. They claim that it took 10 000 years for Aborigines to move from the northern coast to south-western and south-eastern Australia. They also argue that 50 000 years ago the world's sea level was 150 metres lower and consequently the journey through the Indonesian archipelago would have been a relatively easy combination of walking and short boat trips.

The first inhabitants could not have realised that they had arrived on a continent, not just another island. In fact at that time it is likely that Australia, Papua New Guinea and Tasmania were all joined.

For the next 55 000 years the Aborigines moved right across the continent actively hunting and gathering and establishing themselves in semi-permanent settlements in areas where the food was rich and plentiful. Recent archaeological work has provided a number of hints as to the progress the people made across the continent.

The oldest known tools to be discovered probably date from around 38 000 years ago. These were located in the upper reaches of the Swan River in Western Australia. It would seem that at this point Aborigines had moved down through Western Australia and were living in areas where the winters would have been much colder than they are today.

One of the most significant of all early Aboriginal archaeological sites is that at Lake Mungo in far western New South Wales. This dates from around 30–32 000 years ago. The significance of this site is that it suggests a range of complex social behaviour. There is evidence of the use of ochre in ritual burial at the site. In the book Bruising the Red Earth, Antonia Sagona writes: 'At Lake Mungo, New South Wales, a male skeleton (Mungo III) of delicate build was found stained red with haemetite. The skeleton was found in a shallow grave, placed on its back and turned slightly to the right so that its head rested on the shoulder, the hands were clasped resting on the pelvis, and the legs were slightly bent at the knees. Dated to 28 000 BC, the Mungo interment attests the only known use of ochre in mortuary practice from a Pleistocene site in Australia.'

Malangerr in the Northern Territory has also been the source of a major archaeological discovery. Stone axe heads dating back to 22 000 BC have been found there. These are some of the oldest axe heads found on earth.

Discoveries at a number of other sites have given an indication of the spread of Aborigines throughout the Australian continent. Archaeologists have found evidence of stone tools at Keilor in Victoria which date back to 32 000 BC. Around 28 000 BC there is evidence at Devils Lair in Western Australia that Aborigines were living off the flora and fauna of the area. By 24 000 BC Aborigines were fishing for yabbies and other fresh-water life on the shores of Tandou Lake in New South Wales and

there is evidence of Aboriginal settlement in Tasmania.

Around 20 000 BC archaeological finds suggest that most of the continent was inhabited and that the Aborigines were actively using the local resources in creative ways. There is evidence of settlement in Tasmania (Kutinkina Cave in Tasmania is reputedly the southern-most ice age site in the world), on the Nullarbor Plain, at Mount Newman in Western Australia, in northern Queensland and in Arnhem Land. In these widely varying sites evidence has been found of flint mining, the use of ochre for artistic purposes and the first finger painting on cave walls. It seems from the walls of Koonalda Cave on the Nullarbor Plain that the local Aborigines were painting on the walls.

If this dating is accurate, it means that the Australian Aborigines were expressing themselves artistically 5000 years before Europeans crept into caves in southern France and Spain to draw crude images of animals on walls.

By 16 000 BC Aborigines had devised a method of collecting and grinding wild seeds (a technique which survives to the present day). The continent seems to have been well settled by this time. Settlement sites range from the Murray River in western New South Wales to the Ord River in far northern Western Australia.

Over the next 18 000 years stone tools became increasing sophisticated and by 1000 AD hook and line fishing, probably learnt from the trepang fishermen and traders from Timor and Indonesia, became commonplace around the coast.

It was also during this period that the narrow land corridor between Australia and New Guinea was cut off by the rising level of the ocean (around 6000 BC) and the Aborigines in Tasmania were no longer capable of moving back to the mainland (4000 BC).

During this time the dingo arrived on the Australian mainland (around 2000 BC) and the remarkable X-ray art, which is such a feature of the caves in Kakadu National Park, became a common feature of Aboriginal art.

By 1788 there were somewhere between 300 000 and one million Aborigines living in Australia. Population densities varied according to the richness of the areas. It is thought that at the time of the arrival of the first Europeans there were about 3000 people living in the Sydney basin (about 1500 on the coast and about the same number on the Cumberland Plain), 4000 in Gippsland, 3500 in Tasmania and as many as 5000 in the south-western corner of Western Australia. They were essentially hunters and gatherers but their lifestyle varied according to the availability of food. The inhabitants of the Sydney basin and the north and south coasts of New South Wales were quite sedentary, while the Wiradjuri, who occupied the south-western slopes of New South Wales from the Blue Mountains to the edges of the Snowy Mountains, led an extremely active life.

Early exploration of the Australian coastline

For most of the nineteenth and twentieth centuries a very Eurocentric view of Australian history prevailed. This view argued that the first explorers to reach Australia were the Portuguese in the sixteenth century. This conveniently ignored the fact that the Chinese had been exploring the area some centuries before the Europeans rounded the Cape of Good Hope. It seems most likely that the first explorer to reach Australia was the Chinese navigator Cheng Ho, who in the early years of the fifteenth century ventured into the Indian Ocean. It is probable that a statue found near the present-day site of Darwin in 1879 was left by Cheng Ho.

A century later, as a result of Bartholomew Diaz rounding the Cape of Good Hope in 1488, European explorers were venturing across the Indian Ocean. In 1514 Antonio de Abreu reached Timor to the north of Australia and there is some evidence that in 1522 Christo de Mendonça reached the north-west coast of Australia.

By 1531 the words *Terra Australis* were appearing on European maps and by 1536 it was commonplace for these maps to indicate the presence

Tasman's carpenter landing at Storm Bay.

of a major landmass to the south of the East Indies. Throughout the sixteenth century, although there is no evidence of any European charting the coasts of Australia, it was widely accepted by cartographers that south of Java there was a substantial landmass.

There seems to be little doubt that the first European to sight Australia was Luis Vaez de Torres who saw Cape York at the northern tip of Queensland in July 1606. The irony of this discovery was that for over a century the Portuguese had been searching for *Terra Australis Incognito* but Torres assumed it (Cape York) was another island and did not investigate further. Later that year when the Dutch explorer Willem Janszoon sailed the Duyfken down the west coast of Cape York he did not realise that he was charting Terra Australis he believed that he was still exploring the coast of New Guinea. Remarkably, one of groups of Aborigines on Cape York still have a story about a strange vessel with sails which moved down the coast.

The first extensive and detailed exploration of the Australian coastline was a mixture of accident and expediency. By 1619 the Dutch had captured the main centre on the island of Java, renamed it Batavia, and established it as the centre of Dutch influence in the East Indies. Seeking an easier route to the East Indies, Dutch sailors decided to let themselves be pushed across the Indian Ocean by the Roaring Forties and when they hit the coast of New Holland all they had to do was turn north and head for Batavia. The inevitable happened: some ships sailed too far east and arrived at the coast of what is now Western Australia.

It was Henderik Brouwer who, in 1610, discovered that the best route from the Cape of Good Hope to Batavia was via the Roaring Forties. Brouwer achieved the crossing of the Indian Ocean and successfully sailed up the coast of Western Australia.

Six years later Dirk Hartog sailed too far and landed at Cape Inscription on 26 October 1616. It was here that Hartog left his famous pewter plate inscribed (in Dutch): '1616. On 25th October there arrived here the ship *Eendraght* of Amsterdam. Supercargo Gilles Miebais of Liege; skipper Dirck Hatichs of Amsterdam. On 27th do. she set sail again for Bantam. Subcargo Jan Stins; upper steersman Pieter Doores of Bil. In the year 1616.'

Two years later both van Hillegom, Captain of the *Zeewolf*, and Jacobsz, Captain of the *Mauritius*, accidentally landed on the coast. In 1619 Commander Frederik de Houtman sighted Rottnest Island.

In 1623 Dutch ships *Pera* and *Arnhem*, under the commands of Dirk Meliszoon and Wellem van Coolsteerdt respectively, charted the west coast of Cape York and the northern coasts of

Arnhem Land. The Gulf of Carpentaria was named after Pieter de Carpentier, Governor-General of the Dutch East Indies.

Four years later Pieter Nuyts sailed along most of the coast of the Great Australian Bight, and in 1629, the survivors of the shipwrecked *Batavia*, which had literally struck the Houtman Abrolhos islands, sailed for 800 kilometres up the Western Australian coast before heading for Java.

The most revered of all the Dutch explorers was Abel Tasman who, on two voyages in 1642 and 1644, discovered Van Diemen's Land and explored large sections of the northern coastline of the continent. Tasman is credited with the discovery that Australia was not connected to Papua New Guinea and with giving the continent the name 'New Holland'.

The Dutch continued to explore the Western Australian coastline for the next century but they made no attempt to establish an outpost there. The numerous Dutch shipwrecks led to many important voyages of exploration. After the sinking of the *De Ridderschap van Holland* in 1694, Willem de Vlamingh went in search of survivors and discovered Rottnest Island, explored up to 80 kilometres inland, and found Dirk Hartog's pewter plate.

The first Englishmen to set foot on Australian soil was the pirate William Dampier who landed on the Western Australian coast in 1688 and 1699. His best-selling account of his first voyage, *A New Voyage Round the World*, had little to say in Australia's favour and probably dissuaded the British from further exploration of the country. He described the Aborigines as 'the miserablest people on earth' and his description of the climate and terrain appeared in his log as 'we Anchor'd at three several Places, and stay'd at the first of them (on the W. side of the Bay) till the 11th. During which time we searched about, as I said, for fresh Water, digging Wells, but to no purpose.' These were hardly descriptions to encourage further exploration or possible settlement.

The final act in the early exploration of Australia started in 1768 when Captain James Cook, commanding HM Barque *Endeavour*, was sent to the South Seas to observe the transit of Venus and explore the 'Great South Land'. On

Captain Cook off the Glasshouse Mountains.

Cook landing at Botany Bay.

20 April 1770 Zachary Hicks, the First Lieutenant on the ship, sighted the coast of Australia. Cook sailed up the coast for the next four months and on 22 August 1770, on Possession Island, he claimed all the eastern coast for King George III and named it New South Wales.

Nine years later Sir Joseph Banks recommended Botany Bay as a suitable site for a penal colony and in 1786 the British Government authorised the sending of convicts to New South Wales.

The first settlement at Sydney Cove

King George had no doubt about the function of the first European colony on Australian soil. In his speech to the British Parliament in January 1787 he referred to the proposal to send an expedition to Botany Bay as another attempt to 'remove the inconvenience which arose from the crowded state of the gaols in different parts of the Kingdom'. It was hardly the kind of fulsome and enthusiastic description which would bring hope to those who, on 13 May 1787, set sail from Portsmouth. The first fleet consisted of eleven ships: two escorts, HMS *Sirius*, commanded by Governor Arthur Phillip, and HMS *Supply*; six transport ships, *Alexander, Friendship, Scarborough, Charlotte, Lady Penrhyn* and *Prince of Wales*; and three storeships, *Fishburn, Borrowdale* and *Golden Grove*. They carried 759 convicts, twenty-three of them died during the voyage and six children were born. After a journey of nine months, 1030 people landed, 736 of them were convicts.

The site for the settlement was to be Botany Bay. On 18 January Governor Phillip reached the bay on HMS *Supply*. The lack of good, fresh water made the site unsuitable and Phillip proceeded immediately to examine Port Jackson, a short distance to the north. It was, in Phillip's famous expression, 'the finest harbour in the world' and so, by 26 January the entire fleet had moved north and the colony of Sydney had begun.

The early sequence of events was a mixture of decorum and necessity. On 26 January the British flag was raised at Sydney Cove and a few days later the official documents formally appointing Phillip as Governor and formally establishing the colony of New South Wales were read to all members of the expedition. Phillip spoke to the convicts and told them that he hoped the new colony would bring them 'reformation, happiness, and prosperity'.

The first problem, and the one that would come to obsess the early governors, was food. By nineteenth-century standards the convicts had been well fed on the journey to Australia. They had been given 3 quarts (3.4 litres) of water per day and their weekly food rations included 7 pounds (3 kilograms) of biscuit, 2 pounds (1 kilogram) of salt pork, 4 pounds (2 kilograms) of salt beef, 2 pounds (1 kilogram) of peas, 3 pounds (1.5 kilograms) of oatmeal, 6 ounces (170 grams) of butter, 12 ounces (340 grams) of cheese and H pint (284 millilitres) of vinegar per week.

While this was adequate it was hardly a healthy diet and consequently there was an urgent need to produce fresh foodstuffs so that the diet of everyone in the colony could be improved.

Captain Cook proclaiming New South Wales a British possession, Botany Bay, 1770.

To compound the problem the authorities in England had badly underestimated the difficulty of agricultural activity in the area around Sydney Cove. Not only were there few tools but most of the convicts had been urban dwellers and their agricultural ability was restricted. The British authorities had omitted to ensure that skilled labour was on the ships.

Determined to give the new colony every opportunity to succeed, Governor Phillip quickly established other colonies in the area and on 14 February Lieutenant Philip Gidley King, who was accompanied by fifteen convicts and six soldiers, sailed to Norfolk Island with a view to growing crops and harvesting native flax.

Necessity drove the early colony. By July a number of crudely made huts and storehouses had been completed and a Government House (a cottage rather than a gracious dwelling) was being constructed on the hill above the cove. By this time a brick kiln had been built and bricks were being made.

Nothing went smoothly for the early colony. On 30 May two convicts, William Okey and Samuel Davis, were killed by Aborigines while gathering rushes at Rushcutters Bay. While it was an isolated incident it did indicate a certain level of friction between the new settlers and the estimated population of 3000 Aborigines who were living in the Sydney basin at the time.

By July the rations in the colony were running low. In a despatch to the British Under-Secretary of State, Phillip recorded the rations which were being fed to both marines and male convicts—the women were getting two-thirds of these rations: 'Each received 7 pounds of bread or in lieu thereof 7 pounds of flour, 7 pounds of beef or in lieu thereof pork, 3 pints of pease, 6 ounces of butter.'

By September the situation was so bad that the last cow had been killed for meat and the HMS Sirius had been despatched to Cape Town to bring back any food they could get. The following May it returned with 6.5 tonnes of flour. It had circumnavigated the world in the Roaring Forties.

On 2 November, in another attempt to secure

Sydney Cove, 1788.

the future of the colony, Phillip sent a party of marines and ten convicts to develop a farm at Rose Hill near the present-day site of Parramatta.

In spite of this tentative start the colony slowly began to take root. Phillip was an enthusiastic explorer and, in the space of a year, he had carried out expeditions to the foothills of the Blue Mountains, to the shores of Broken Bay in the north, and to Botany Bay where he explored the Cooks, Georges and the Woronora rivers.

The quality of life in the colony began to improve in 1789. Government House was completed; on 4 June some convicts performed George Farquhar's comedy *The Recruiting Officer*; and in October a boat was built to carry supplies up the Parramatta River from Sydney Cove to the settlement at Rose Hill.

In spite of this apparent optimism food was still the colony's grand obsession. In November 1789 supplies were so low that everyone had their limited rations reduced to two-thirds.

Mercifully, on 21 November, Phillip gave the convict James Ruse 2 acres (3.8 hectares) at Rose Hill. He also supplied him with seed, livestock and suitable farming equipment. By December the farms at Rose Hill had produced 200 bushels of wheat and 60 bushels of barley. However, this was only a temporary relief and by January the colony's food supply was so small that everyone was put on half rations.

By April the food situation was so bad that Phillip told his officers and administrators that only six weeks rations remained. Rations were reduced even more and the whole colony focussed on catching fish in the harbour and trying to trap kangaroos and wallabies in the hinterland. Convicts who stole food were being sentenced to 2000 lashes.

On 3 June, after one convict had died from starvation, the Second Fleet sailed through the heads. There were a number of store ships and thus adequate supplies to save the colony from starvation. With the Second Fleet came instructions to settle the land as quickly as possible and to produce food to feed the colony by any possible means.

The first two years had been extremely difficult but the colony had survived. On 25 February 1791, a little over two years after Phillip had raised the flag in Sydney Cove, James Ruse announced that his small farm at Rose Hill was producing

enough food to feed himself and his wife, proving that it was possible to survive in the Sydney basin. The colony now had some genuine hope.

Exploration and expansion of the new continent

It would seem that Australia's first European settlers were a curious and adventurous lot. From the moment they arrived at Botany Bay and Sydney Cove they were eager to push into the hinterland and explore the vast unknown which lay beyond the shoreline and the sand dunes.

On one level they were riding a wave of European exploration which had started in the fifteenth century and which had effectively crossed every ocean and explored every continent. On another level, with the journey from England taking up to six months, there was an urgent need to find fertile soils and verdant pastures so that the colony could become self-sufficient.

It was inevitable that Arthur Phillip, his soldiers and convicts would wonder what lay beyond the horizon. Some convicts, driven more by optimism than reality, believed that they could walk from Sydney to Batavia. Some even believed that a white settlement existed beyond the mountains. They escaped from Sydney Cove only to die in the foothills of the Blue Mountains or to be befriended by local Aborigines.

In March 1788 Phillip and a small party had reached the Pittwater area of Broken Bay and by April the northern shore of Sydney Harbour had been explored. But the real source of fascination were the mountains to the west of the settlement which, on a clear day, looked remarkably blue.

The first twenty-five years of settlement saw only small-scale, land-based explorations. In 1789 expeditions led by Phillip and Watkin Tench discovered the Hawkesbury and Nepean river system on the edge of the Sydney basin. In 1797 a group of shipwreck survivors walked 640 kilometres up the coast towards Sydney from Bass Strait. In the same year Lieutenant John Shortland discovered the Hunter River north of Port Jackson. Later in the decade two parties headed south-west from Sydney and reached as far as the present site of Goulburn.

The real journeys of exploration occurred after 1813 when Blaxland, Wentworth and Lawson crossed the Blue Mountains. Their successful expedition was the culmination of attempts to cross the range which had started as early as 1789.

In the next decade a series of expeditions left Sydney to explore the lands beyond the mountains. In 1815 a road over the Blue Mountains was built and George Evans, who had been exploring beyond the mountains, headed south from the village of Bathurst and reached the Lachlan River.

In 1817 and 1818 John Oxley pushed south and nearly reached the Murrumbidgee River, then headed north and reached the present site of Port Macquarie. In 1819 John Howe successfully travelled overland to the Hunter Valley and in 1823 Captain Mark Currie explored the Lake George area near present-day Canberra and pushed on until he reached the Murrumbidgee River.

If the 1810s had seen explorers stay relatively close to Port Jackson the 1820s and 1830s saw them reach into areas which would subsequently become parts of Queensland and South Australia. In 1824 Hamilton Hume and William Hovell explored from south of Sydney through to

Oxley exploring the Macquarie River.

Captain Charles Sturt.

the Western Port district of Victoria. They had hoped to reach Port Phillip but they miscalculated.

Three years later, in 1827, Allan Cunningham headed north from the Upper Hunter Valley and reached the Liverpool Plains and the rich Darling Downs. All these explorers had been primarily concerned with finding and opening up good grazing land so that the inhabitants could be fed. They were people committed to practical exploration. In the 1830s such exploration gave way to journeys which were either to answer vexing questions like 'Why do so many of the rivers in New South Wales flow inland?', or to achieve status by being the first person to traverse the country from south to north.

In 1828–29 Charles Sturt, who wanted to know where the rivers flowed, explored the Macquarie, Darling, Castlereagh and Bogan. The following year he followed the Murrumbidgee downstream until he reached the Murray. He followed the Murray until it joined the Darling and then continued until it emptied into Lake Alexandrina in South Australia.

In 1831 Major Thomas Mitchell explored the rivers in the north-west of New South Wales and in 1836 he made an epic journey through western New South Wales and north-western Victoria where, after crossing numerous rivers, he came across rich pastoral land which he named 'Australia Felix'.

The only other major exploration before 1840 occurred in 1839 when Angus McMillan and Paul Strzelecki pushed down through the Snowy Mountains and opened up the rich pasturelands of western Victoria.

These early explorations concentrated on New South Wales and reached out to the limits of the state. In the following decades the true vastness of the country was explored. Ludwig Leichhardt travelled from Jimour in Queensland across to Port Essington (Darwin) in the Northern Territory. A. C. Gregory made epic journeys through outback South Australia and across the Northern Territory to the Victoria River, and the ill-fated Edmond Kennedy struggled through dense tropical rainforest from Rockingham Bay up the coast of Cape York.

Throughout the 1850s, 1860s and 1870s major explorations occurred. Burke and Wills and John McDouall Stuart both crossed the continent from north to south. E. J. Eyre crossed the Great Australian Bight and John Forrest, Alexander Forrest, Edward Giles, A. C. and F. T. Gregory explored vast inland areas of Western Australia.

Slowly the continent was opened up. The dreams of vast pastures and of inland seas disap-

Sturt on the Murrumbidgee.

peared as explorer after explorer found that the inland reality was desert, heat, flies, disease and genuine hardship.

The period of exploration lasted for a century. By the end of the nineteenth century the inhabitants of Australia had a detailed, if not comprehensive, understanding of the continent. They realised that clinging to the coast was a necessity rather than a desirable option for the inland was such a vast emptiness.

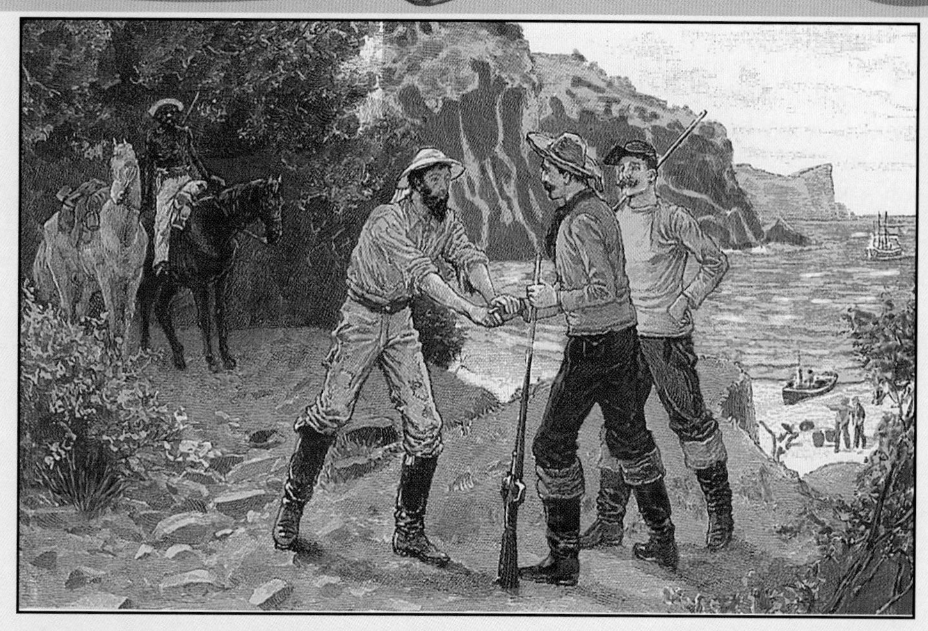

Meeting of Eyre with French whalers.

The creation of Australia's states and territories

In terms of its states and colonies Australia has changed its internal boundaries twelve times since the British government gave Captain Arthur Phillip his commission in 1786. In the original commission received by Phillip the continent, which at the time was still a blurry and inaccurate outline on a map, was divided down the 135th meridian of east longitude. This basically meant that all of Australia east of a line which ran from Arnhem Land down to the eastern edge of the Great Australian Bight (and which included both Van Diemen's Land and New Zealand) was known as New South Wales. The area to the west of the 135th meridian was not claimed.

Fear of possible French and Dutch settlement drove much of decision-making in early Australian history. By 1824, with the establishment of the brief and unsuccessful settlement of Fort Dundas on Melville Island the boundary of New South Wales was extended to the 129th parallel. Interestingly, this is the oldest permanent artificial state boundary in Australia. When the British claimed Western Australia in 1829 they defined it by the 129th parallel and that is still the state's eastern boundary.

In 1825 Van Diemen's Land was constituted as a separate colony. The territory of Van Diemen's Land included all the islands south of Wilsons Promontory including Macquarie Island which had been annexed by the British because of its popularity as a destination for whalers and sealers. The main island continued to be known as Van Diemen's Land until it was changed to Tasmania in 1855.

The next colony to be carved from greater New South Wales was South Australia which was created on 15 August 1834 by King William IV. Like New South Wales and Western Australia its boundaries were simply lines drawn on maps with no consideration to terrain (which was not known at the time) or natural features. Thus, the first South Australia was simply defined as all that territory bounded by the 132nd and 141st meridians of east longitude and by the 26th parallel south and the southern coastline. In 1861 the western boundary was extended to the 129th parallel so that it formed a border with Western Australia and from 1863, until it was taken over by the new Federal Government in 1911, the Northern Territory was included as part of the state.

Few Australians realise that New Zealand remained a kind of informal dependency of the colony of New South Wales until 1840. In that year it became a formal dependency but the formal connection was shortlived because the following year it was proclaimed as a separate colony.

The goldrushes saw the most dramatic changes

in the evolution of Australia's states. The rapidly expanding population along the continent's eastern seaboard meant that it became impossible for the growing goldrush towns to be administered from Sydney. Also the new goldrush ports of Melbourne, and later the towns along the north Queensland coast, could not be sensibly controlled from Sydney.

In 1851 the colony of Victoria was constituted. It had been known as the Port Phillip District. The definition of the colony reached beyond simple straight lines drawn on a map. Victoria was formally 'bounded on the north and north-east by a straight line drawn from Cape Howe to the nearest source of the River Murray, and thence by the course of that river to the eastern boundary of the colony of South Australia.' It was a colony with a natural boundary.

The last state to emerge was Queensland which was finally granted an independent administration on 6 June 1859. It effectively carved the northern two-thirds off New South Wales.

In broad terms it was all the land from the coast to the 141st meridian of east longitude and all the land north of the 29th parallel with the easterly-most section of the border following the course of the Macpherson, Dumaresq and Macintyre rivers.

All that was left to complete the picture of modern Australia was for the Australian Capital Territory, a strange combination of 2360 square kilometres in New South Wales and 72 square kilometres at Jervis Bay (in case a port was required), to be handed over to the new Federal government in 1911, and for the Northern Territory to be moved from South Australia to the Commonwealth in 1911, be carved up into North and Central Australia between 1926–31, and eventually be granted its own elected administration in 1976.

The evolution of Australia's states and territories was a mixture of cartographic whims and the changing nature of Australia's population in the nineteenth century. It is remarkable that with such flimsy reasons for division that, in less than one hundred years, the states began to assert their own identity.

The goldrushes change Australia forever

'Put it away Mr Clarke or we shall all have our throats cut!' the New South Wales Governor Sir George Gipps is supposed to have said when a geologist, the Reverend W. B. Clarke, first showed him some gold which he had found in a creek near Lithgow in New South Wales. The year was 1844 and the Governor of the Colony of New South Wales was worried that a public announcement of the discovery of gold, especially in a colony where the majority of the residents were convicts, would cause violence and chaos.

If the government didn't want a goldrush it was certain that the squatters and farmers didn't. The last thing they wanted was farm labourers leaving their lowly paid jobs to try their luck on the goldfields.

So pressure from the government and rural interests managed to keep the secret of Australia's gold away from the public for twenty-eight years. The first discovery of gold had occurred as early as 1823 when J. McBrien, a government surveyor, found gold in the Fish River near Bathurst. Then in 1839 Peter Strzelecki found gold near Hartley.

Transportation to the colony ended in 1840 and by the end of the decade the fears of the violence that a goldrush might produce had subsided. A mass exodus of the population to California searching for gold caused the New South Wales Government, under Governor FitzRoy, to institute a policy of gold exploration in 1849.

The beginning of the Australian goldrushes occurred when Edward Hargraves, after eighteen months working on the Californian goldfields, returned to Australia with a belief that the area around Bathurst and Orange might contain gold. On 12 February 1851, at the junction of Summer Hill Creek and Lewis Ponds Creek, Hargraves and a colleague, John Lister, successfully panned

gold. In April, Lister and two brothers, James and William Tom, found gold at Ophir. In May 1851 Hargraves took 120 grams of gold to Sydney and showed it to the Colonial Secretary and on 14 May the gold discovery was announced. Within days men were pouring into the Ophir area. The goldrush had started.

The success of the New South Wales goldfields caused a rush of people from Victoria to New South Wales. To stop this a Gold Discovery Committee was formed and £200 was offered to anyone who could find gold in Victoria.

The Gold Discovery Committee did not have to wait long. Only six weeks after the Ophir announcement James Esmond found substantial gold deposits near Clunes and within the next eight months the vast deposits at Ballarat and Bendigo had been discovered.

Inevitably the squatters' worst fears became reality. Farm labourers, indeed anyone who was touched by gold fever, simply threw down their tools and using any available transport headed for the goldfields. Mostly the prospectors simply walked. Often they pushed their equipment in wheelbarrows. Only the affluent went to the diggings on horseback or in a coach. Usually the roads they travelled were little more than bush tracks which were dusty in summer and impossibly muddy in wet weather.

Prior to 1851 the Australian population was increasing in a slow and measured way. Australia had an average of 12 000 free immigrants a year from 1832 to 1842. After the discovery of gold the population of the country soared. From 1851 to 1861 the population trebled. In Victoria alone the population rose from 80 000 to 500 000. In September 1851, 19 000 people landed at Melbourne. In 1852, 95 000 people arrived in Australia.

It was common at this time for everybody who could make it to Australia to come and try their luck on the goldfields. The first to arrive were the experienced miners who were happy to leave the nearly exhausted Californian goldfields.

Interestingly, the majority of immigrants were English, Scottish and Irish. It is true that virtually every nationality on earth could be found on the goldfields but for the duration of the goldrushes the English, Scottish and Irish were by far the largest groups.

Fossicking

The Chinese, who were later to provoke considerable anger on the goldfields, did not start arriving in substantial numbers until as late as the mid-1850s. The first group, many of whom had come from the Californian goldfields, blended in with the rich racial mix on the diggings. Then in 1854–55, in a period of eighteen months, 18 000 Chinese arrived. The antagonism from European and Australian diggers was immediate. By the late 1850s the total number of Chinese on the goldfields had risen to 40 000 and they were establishing themselves as a separate community.

The attitude of European and Australian miners was that the Chinese wasted water, reworked other miners' shafts, smoked opium and gambled too much. The Chinese looked upon the Europeans with equal disdain.

These feelings of animosity finally burst into a series of riots at Bendigo and Buckland Valley in Victoria and Lambing Flat in New South Wales.

On the road to the diggings.

The result was that the colonies began placing restrictions on the entry of Chinese into Australia. This was the beginning of what would eventually become known as the 'White Australia Policy'.

Although the goldrushes occurred in the 1850s prospectors continued to find new goldfields, particularly in Western Australia and Queensland, from the 1860s to the 1890s.

In Queensland there were a series of goldrushes in the 1870s to places which appeared and disappeared as the miners rushed to the diggings and then rushed on to the next goldfield. Towns like Maytown, Palmer and Croydon briefly enjoyed booms. The more important and long-lasting centres included Gympie, Charters Towers and Mount Morgan.

In Western Australia gold discovery occurred as late as the 1880s and 1890s with lodes being found in the Kimberley and Pilbara regions and major finds in the Kalgoorlie and Coolgardie fields.

The last region of Australia to be mined was the Northern Territory where successful gold discovery peaked in 1894 when over 1 million grams were discovered.

Boom and bust in the 1880s and 1890s

It was inevitable that the incredible boom created by the goldrushes would not last. The goldrushes, particularly in Victoria and New South Wales, had stretched all the existing services and brought unprecedented wealth into the colonies. The population of Australia had grown dramatically in a very short period. In Victoria, for example, the population increased by 114 000 immigrants in the decade between 1881 and 1890. It was obvious that no colony could sustain such a demand on its services.

To compound the problem the wealth generated by the goldrushes had made some people rich and they began to speculate on the development and growth of the cities of Sydney and Melbourne. Whole new suburbs were built, the age of the city high-rise (although it was rarely

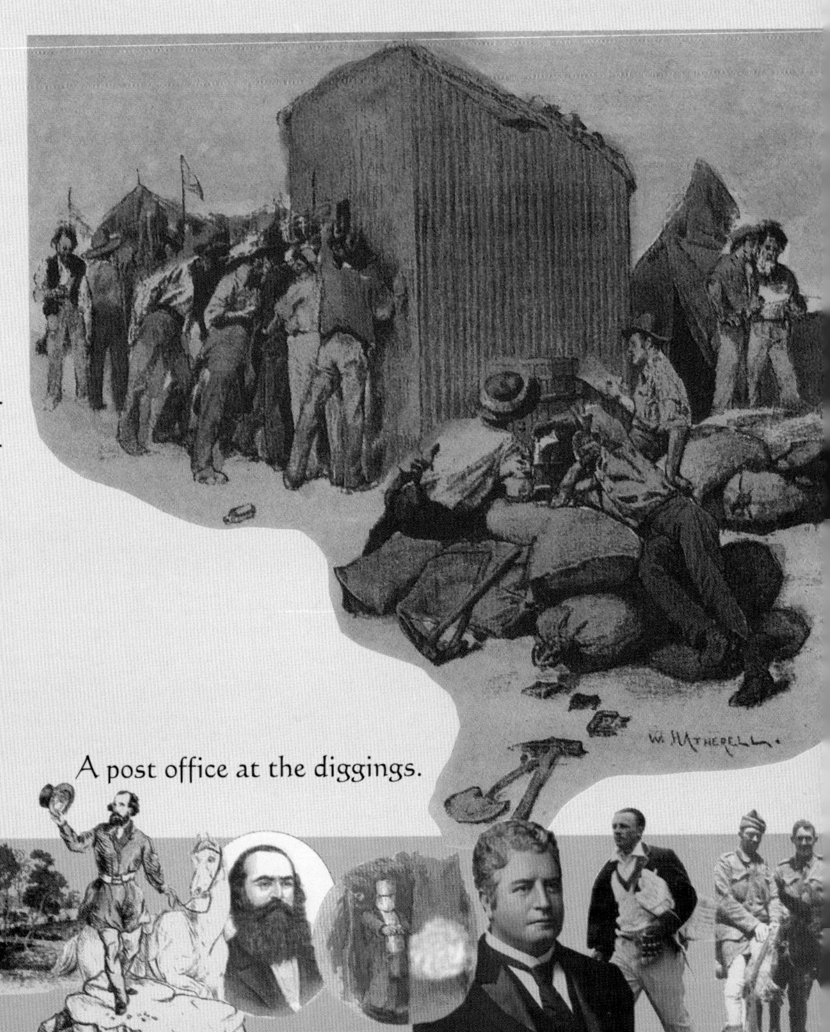

A post office at the diggings.

Timbering a mine.

above four stories) had begun, and the governments, buoyed by their new-found wealth, began to borrow money from British investors to build railways and expand public works.

By the end of the 1880s two forces were at work. There was a great, and unjustified, belief that the rural sector in all the colonies could keep growing indefinitely and land companies and building societies were investing in the future real estate development of the big cities without any real consideration for the economic viability of their projects. It was a time of enthusiastic optimism where the signs of an imminent collapse were simply ignored.

Much of Australia's wealth at this time was determined by the annual wool clip. The country had become the world's largest producer of fine wool and this had produced a certain arrogance. When the wool price began to decline (due largely to competition from other markets) the local graziers and financiers did not heed the warning.

Thus, when wool prices and the housing market collapsed in 1890 the economy was totally unprepared. The result was the collapse of the banking industry and, although it is difficult to measure, it is likely that the 1890s saw the worst depression Australia has ever experienced.

In Victoria in January 1893 two-thirds of all the banks had closed their doors and suspended payments to depositors. The inevitable followed. Bankruptcies were commonplace. The queues of the unemployed grew alarmingly. Business became paralysed and fearful that anything it did may lead to further economic hardship.

The most frightening consequence of the collapse was the way it exacerbated class conflict. Graziers, trying to deal with falling wool prices and the collapse of the banks, decided that their workers would have to bear the full brunt of the depression. Disheartened rural workers started to leave the country and move either to the cities or to return to their countries of origin. The population of Victoria actually dropped during the depression.

To make matters worse Australia experienced an eight-year drought during the period. It was clear that the rural sector, which had been so vibrant before the depression, was likely to be the country's saviour but, with a drought, it had little ability to regenerate.

The country slowly pulled itself out of the crisis. The economy's dependence on wool was broken as farmers looked towards meat and dairy products. At the same time the discovery of silver and lead at Broken Hill and the rich gold finds on the Kalgoorlie–Coolgardie fields ensured that by the turn of the century the economies of the colonies were dragging themselves back to their pre-depression levels.

The move towards federation

By the 1890s the inexorable and inevitable movement towards federation was occupying the minds of both politicians and the public. Ideas which had been debated for more than fifty years started to be important on the political agenda and public meetings and conferences began to be held around the country.

An invitation to the Federation Inaugural Celebrations in Sydney, 1901.

In essence, federation reversed a process which had started in 1788 and continued until the 1850s. During this time the coherent, single island continent had been carved up, often at the whim of politicians and cartographers with a map and a ruler, into an ever-increasing number of states. Where once New South Wales had covered two-thirds of the continent, now it was broken up into a number of sparsely-populated colonies.

The foolishness of this fragmentation was recognised as early as 1846 when, in the New South Wales Legislative Council, the notion of some sort of legislation which linked the colonies was raised. The following year the British Secretary of State for the Colonies argued that some kind of central authority was probably necessary and, in 1851, Governor FitzRoy's responsibilities were expanded from Governor of New South Wales to Governor-General of all Her Majesty's Australian possessions. It was a position which only lasted for a decade and fortunately was never seriously tested by FitzRoy or his successor. A hint of the forthcoming battle occurred when both Tasmania and South Australia expressed grave reservations about the possibility of domination by New South Wales and Victoria.

Between 1850 and 1880 the idea of a federation was kept alive by isolated, quixotic politicians who believed in the merit of the idea. William Charles Wentworth was actively involved in the formation of the London-based General Association for the Australian Colonies in the mid-1850s. Select committees were formed by the New South Wales and Victorian parliaments to investigate the problems of establishing a federation. Unfortunately the suspicion and antagonisms which already existed between colonies conspired to scuttle any serious proposals. There is little doubt that a lack of any feeling of national identity combined with local political aspirations worked against any serious movement towards federation.

Inevitably during the 1860s and 1870s the colonies moved further and further apart. Some colonies prospered and others declined. Separate politicians on issues like immigration tariffs and defence began to emerge. Between 1863 and 1880 eight intercolonial conferences were held to resolve these basic issues. Federation had been so comprehensively dropped from the political agenda that it was rarely discussed at these conferences.

Eventually the problems became so great that during the course of the 1880 intercolonial conference Henry Parkes recommended the establishment of a permanent federal council. It was only supported by South Australia, Tasmania and New South Wales. It seemed to fail although, when Germany and France began showing interest in colonising the Pacific, the states that had baulked at a federal council suddenly appreciated its value.

At the time there was a belief that Britain should take a more active role in colonising the Pacific. The major aim of the council was to exert pressure on Britain. In this it was successful and a Federal Council met for the first time in 1886. It continued to meet every two years until federation.

It is one of the ironies of the 'federation process' that Henry Parkes, who had recommended the establishment of the federal council, refused to have anything to do with it, believing it to be flawed and ineffectual.

However, on 24 October 1889 at Tenterfield in northern New South Wales, Parkes addressed a meeting and argued persuasively that Australia

had to develop a national defence force. Historians consider this speech to be the true starting point for the movement which culminated in federation eleven years later.

On 2 March 1891 forty-five delegates from all states gathered in Sydney for the first meeting of the National Australasian Convention. The convention established committees to draft a bill which would create the Commonwealth of Australia. If the political and economic forces had been different the Commonwealth of Australia may have become a reality within eighteen months but a severe depression and the emergence of the Labor Party ensured that it was once again pushed down the agenda.

Ships at Sandridge Pier, Melbourne, c. 1878.

Edmund Barton, who had effectively taken over from Henry Parkes as the federation champion in New South Wales, abandoned the slow parliamentary process and established a number of grassroots 'federal leagues' in towns and cities.

In 1893 a conference of these leagues was held at Corowa, New South Wales. The outcome of this conference was an agreement that each colony should elect representatives who would draw up a federal constitution which, in turn, would be put to a referendum. The breakthrough was that this was a practical way of carrying through the campaign for federation and seeing it resolved by a vote.

There was a mood of change in the air and it was now impossible for any of the state governments to resist. Thus, on 22 March 1897, after enabling legislation had been passed in every state apart from Queensland, the Federal Convention was convened in Adelaide. Two further sessions were held in Sydney and Melbourne in September 1897 and January–February 1898 respectively. By 13 March 1898 a draft constitution had been completed and in early June that same year the voters of New South Wales, Victoria, Tasmania and South Australia went to the polls. The result was 219 712 for federation and 108 363 against with Victoria recording an extraordinary 100 520 for and only 22 099 against.

Unfortunately, the referendum was only narrowly won in New South Wales (71 595 for and 66 228 against) and, given that the parliament had required a minimum of 80 000 votes for federation, the referendum did not pass. The premiers met in Melbourne in early 1899 to discuss possible amendments. Both Western Australia and Queensland were represented at this meeting. Minor changes were made to the draft legislation and during 1899 the states once again voted on the legislation. This time all requirements were satisfied with 377 988 voting for federation and only 141 386 voting against it.

The final process was for the bill to be taken to London where the British parliament had to enact it into legislation. A delegation comprising Edmund Barton, Alfred Deakin, C. C. Kingston, J. R. Dickson and Sir Philip Fysh travelled to London to ensure that the federation bill passed through the British parliament without amendment. At this time Western Australia was still resisting federation. It requested that the British parliament incorporate its amendments but the parliament refused. The bill remained relatively unchanged.

In July 1900 Western Australia voted to join the federation. On 17 September 1900 Queen Victoria signed a proclamation approving the establishment of the federation on the first day of

the new century and thus, on 1 January 1901 the Commonwealth of Australia became a reality.

Developing a concept of nationhood

World War I lasted from 1914 to 1918 and saw some 59 340 Australians die on foreign soils thousands of miles from their homeland. In spite of its distance from Australian shores, and the sense that Australian troops were fighting the wars of others, it is within the larger context of the war, and particularly the near-massacre of Australian troops suffered at Gallipoli, that particularly vital elements of the Australian character were wrought. Indeed it can be argued that those elements of our national identity which hover between myth and reality—the bronzed Anzac, independence, a natural sporting ability, an innate desire for fair play, a belief that we live in the lucky country, a healthy disrespect for authority, and a near-worship of individual enterprise—were actually forged on the battlefields of Europe and the Middle East.

It is easy to forget, however, that this emergent sense of nationhood had actually started before World War I. It seemed as though the moment people made the decision to become 'Australians' and create a federation that a sense of pride in country was immediately instilled. Australians seemed to see themselves as new and bursting with enthusiasm. It is hardly surprising then that when a contributor, obviously of British sympathies, wrote an article to *The Lone Hand* in 1910 declaring that Australians abroad were not liked because they were 'provincial, unreliable and have an irrepressible tendency to blow, brag and skite', he was greeted by a barrage of proud self-justification.

One writer summed up Australian pride when, replying to this perceived slur on Australian nationhood, he asked indignantly: 'Did Melba, or Ada Crossley, or Amy Castles prove "unreliable" when their voices were taken in hand? ... Is Brennan's torpedo and mono-rail any the worse for having been invented by an Australian? And what of Norman Brookes, who recently won the world's championship at lawn tennis? ... and in cricket and football have Australians proved their unreliability against England's best teams? ... did Lord Kitchener suppose them to be "unreliable" in the war, when he had every troop of them in the fighting line, whilst 90,000 British regulars, militia and South African volunteers defended the lines of communications? It almost seems that the Australian has a pretty fair right to an "irrepressible tendency" towards bragging.'

There was a wonderful buoyant sense of self-confidence, naïveté and optimism. The country sent men off to war because it thought of England as the 'Mother Country' and saw local obligations in terms of a kind of family commitment. Australians became inordinately excited at the aerial exploits of local aviators and of sportspeople.

This was a period of great achievements on a number of fronts. In 1912 John Flynn founded the Australian Inland Mission and, in that same year, Sir Douglas Mawson explored the icy wastes of Antarctica.

As a young geologist, Mawson had travelled to Antarctica in 1907 with Ernest Shackleton. By 1911 he had mustered sufficient funds and support to lead his own, and Australia's first, expedition to the southern polar region. With his two companions, one a German aristocrat, Xavier Mertz, and a member of the British fusiliers, Lieutenant Belgrave Ninnis, Mawson planned to explore 2400 kilometres of Antarctic coastline. Some 515 kilometres from the base camp Ninnis, along with the good supplies and vital equipment, disappeared into a crevasse. Mertz and Mawson decided return to base while trying to survive on dog meat, but the meat contained toxic levels of vitamin A which led to madness and death. When Mertz died, Mawson, driven only by instinct, continued across the frozen wastes for 160 kilometres, only to arrive at his base camp the day his ship left. He had to wait a year before he could return to Australia where he became a national hero.

There seemed to be no end to the levels of con-

fidence which existed at the time. In 1912 the then Prime Minister, Andrew Fisher, announced that the American Walter Burley Griffin was the winner of the worldwide competition to design a federal capital for the new nation of Australia. The flamboyant Minister of Home Affairs, King O'Malley, announced, 'This must be the finest capital in the world'.

The culture of the pre-war period was equally important in the way it defined the nation. The films of the period included *On Our Selection* which appeared in 1912 and *The Sentimental Bloke* in 1919. In fact C. J. Dennis' book, *The Sentimental Bloke*, had been published in October 1915 and had sold an incredible 66 148 copies by March 1917.

The pre-war period also saw the production of a range of important, defining works of literature. Henry Lawson wrote *Mateship* (1911) and *Backblock Ballads* (1913); C. J. Dennis followed his 1914 success *(The Sentimental Bloke)* with *The Moods of Ginger Mick* (1915) and the unofficial national anthem *The Australaise* (1915); Banjo Paterson published *Saltbush Bill* in 1917; and in that same year Henry Handel Richardson published *Australia Felix*, the first volume of her epic trilogy *The Fortunes of Richard Mahony*.

Musically, Nellie Melba (soon to be Dame Nellie Melba) strode through the pre-war years like the diva and prima donna that she undoubtedly was. In 1911 she toured Australia with the Irish tenor John McCormack; in 1915 she set up a singing school in Melbourne, and by 1918 she had been made a Dame Commander of the British Empire.

This was also a period of extraordinary Australian sporting prowess. In 1910 Frank Beaurepaire (who later made his fortune in motor-car tyres) toured Europe and competed in forty-eight races against the finest swimmers of the time. He raced over distances ranging from 100 yards to one mile and he won every race. In the same year an Australian professional runner, Jack Donaldson, ran the 100 yards in 9⅜ seconds. His achievement was so exceptional that his record was not beaten until 1948.

In 1912 T. J. Matthews took two hat tricks in one Test match in South Africa—a feat unequalled since. In 1912, 1913 and 1914 Bill Longworth won and held every New South Wales and Australian swimming title from 200 yards to one mile and in 1914 Norman Brookes won both the Wimbledon singles and doubles.

Among the sporting achievements there were also events which were to become part of the country's mythology. Les Darcy, the boxer from Maitland, may have become one of the world's great heavyweight boxers but the war deprived him of worthwhile opponents. Snowy Baker, the strongman archetype of the 'bronzed Aussie he-man', became a role model for Australian males. Fanny Durack won the 100 metres freestyle at the 1912 Stockholm Olympics thus becoming the first sportswoman to win an Olympic gold medal. At Freshwater Beach in Sydney Duke Kahanamoku introduced Australians to the mysteries of surfboard riding and Prince Wickyama (known in Australia as Alick Whickham) from the Solomon Islands, introduced the nation to the swimming stroke which became known as the Australian Crawl.

World War I and the Anzacs

In the absence of any internal wars Australia has seen the experience of the two World Wars as hugely significant. In the case of World War I it did much to define the character of the nation.

If there is a theme which is common to all the wars involving Australians, it is the theme of departure. Wars have always been fought overseas and consequently the most potent images of war are images of wives and sweethearts waving farewell to troopships and ecstatic relatives greeting the returning warriors.

World War I, or the Great War, saw 329 000 soldiers leave the country. In the hearts and minds of Australians it was a confusing war. The posters and the politicians demanded unflinching patriotism and yet only one in twelve went to the war. Twice the Australian electorate rejected

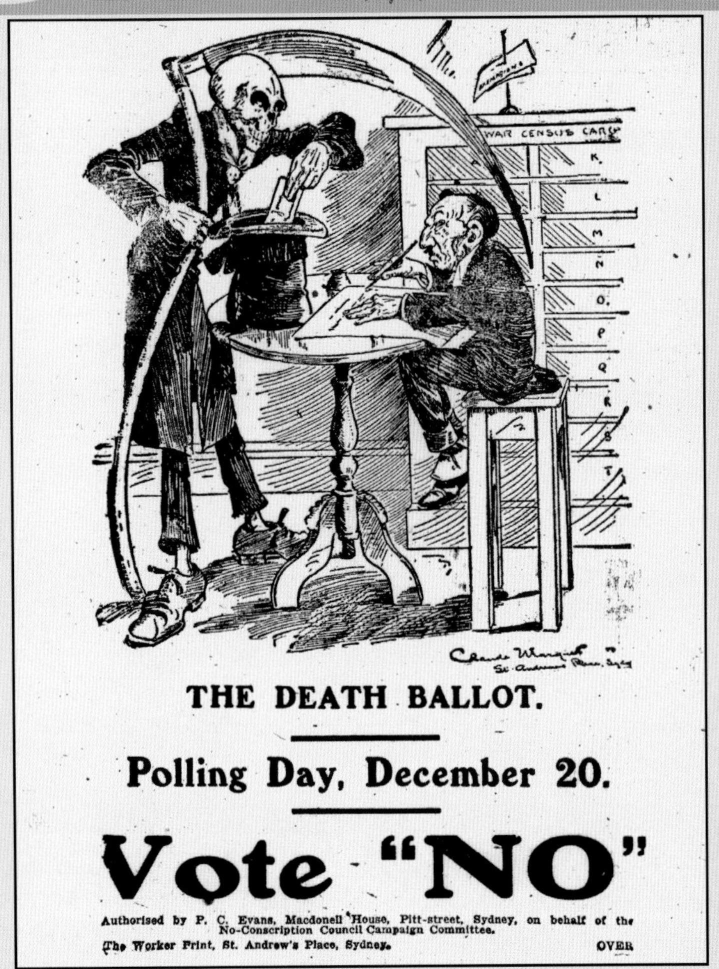

WAR CENSUS CARDS
THE DEATH BALLOT.
Polling Day, December 20.
Vote "NO"
Authorised by P. C. Evans, Macdonell House, Pitt-street, Sydney, on behalf of the No-Conscription Council Campaign Committee.
The Worker Print, St. Andrew's Place, Sydney.
OVER

A newspaper advertisement to encourage people to vote against conscription.

Billy Hughes' impassioned pleas for conscription powers.

For all this ambivalence, the war did create some remarkably potent myths. In the blood and destruction of Gallipoli, the image of the fearless Anzac, the jaunting slouch-hatted digger, the ever-optimistic patriot was forged. In the deserts of Egypt the legendary bushman's prowess with the horse was put to the test by the Australian Light Horse Brigade. At Gallipoli, a curly-headed larrikin named John Simpson found a donkey and transported hundreds of wounded soldiers from the front line back to the beach. After twenty-five days he was a legend—and he was dead. The nation's courage was measured in terms of sixty-six Victoria Crosses.

With war in Europe becoming inevitable, Andrew Fisher dissolved the federal parliament and declared a general election but, before the election could be held, Britain declared war on Germany (4 August 1914) and the war became the central election issue. Anticipating the outbreak of hostilities, Andrew Fisher proudly declared on 1 August:

> Turn your eyes to the European situation and give the kindest feelings towards the mother country at this time. I sincerely hope that international arbitration will avail before Europe is convulsed in the greatest war of any time ... But should the worst happen after everything has been done that honour will permit, Australia will stand by our own to help and defend her to our last man and our last shilling.

The government acted swiftly and the nature of Australia's military commitment to Britain was clearly established. The entire Australian navy was transferred to Britain and placed at Britain's disposal. On the voyage to England HMAS *Sydney* received two distress signals from the telegraph station on Cocos Island. Speeding towards the island, the *Sydney* caught the German battle cruiser *Emden* with half her crew ashore and pinned her between the island and the sea. In the battle which ensued the *Sydney* forced the *Emden* aground on a coral reef. It was one of the Allies' first sea victories. The *Sydney* and the rest of the naval convoy then continued on to Britain.

Apart from transferring its navy to Britain, Australia also established the Australian Flying Corps, seized the German south-west Pacific territories and, under Sir William Birdwood, formed the Australian and New Zealand Corps (ANZAC).

In 1915 the first Anzacs landed at Gallipoli and some 10 000 of them died in what was to be a pointless campaign. That same year no fewer than 250 000 Australians enlisted for service overseas—but this, according to the new Prime Minister, William Morris Hughes, was still not enough. Hughes introduced a 'Call to Arms' encouraging men to enlist in the military forces.

By 1916 Australia was deeply involved in the

war in Europe. Thousands of men were fighting on the Somme, the Australian Light Horse had been committed to Syria and Palestine and the first Australian Flying Unit was being transported by ship to Egypt.

Hughes decided that conscription was essential. On 30 August 1916 he announced that a referendum on conscription would be held on 28 October. In the end the conscription referendum was lost due in part to an active anti-conscription campaign by the major unions and, so folklore has it, strong lobbying by soldiers at the front who didn't want their mates to suffer in the way they had. (In truth the soldiers at the front voted 'Yes' by a small majority.) The 'No' vote won by the slender margin of seventy-two thousand.

In May 1917 Hughes called a Federal election and won on a 'Win the War' platform. Once again Hughes went to the people to try and gain conscription powers and once again he was defeated—this time with twice the 'No' vote he had received the year before. Hughes resigned after his referendum defeat but in the absence of another leader he was re-elected.

The war finally came to an end in 1918. Some 59 340 Australians had been killed, 166 819 wounded and 329 000 had served overseas. Hughes and the war had decimated the Labor Party and it was in such an environment that Earl Page founded the Country Party.

At home, the war had a strange effect. Cut off from European imports, Australia was forced to manufacture its own goods. In 1915 BHP opened a blast furnace at Newcastle and by 1916 Wunderlich were manufacturing three million terracotta roof tiles (replacing the tiles previously imported from France) and, as the advertisements said, 'painting the town red'.

For most Australians, the war was something far away. It is interesting that on the night of 11 November 1918, the night peace was declared, the singer Gladys Moncrieff was performing in Sydney. The performance was interrupted to announce the cessation of hostilities and, at the finale of the first act, white pigeons were released from the stage.

Between the Wars

Though the war had seemed far away to Australians, there were still many who had lost loved ones or who found themselves coping with the task of rehabilitating those who did return.

Aboriginal society was in crisis and the government attempted to solve the problems of social disintegration with the Ordinance of the Northern Territory legislation in 1918. It was a draconian concept of separateness which in the end did little to help those aboriginals most at risk and in the end proved unworkable. though it remained in place until 1953.

The influenza epidemic of 1919 took a huge toll in lives and convenience. Because the disease was so virilent, restrictions were put in place requiring people to wear masks in public and forced theatres, racecourses and schools to close. People were not allowed to stay in bars for more than five minutes and Church services were restricted to forty-five minutes with people sitting one metre apart. By the end of the year it was over but in the process few people had avoided some kind of contact with the disease. In all 11 552 Australians died in the epidemic.

From 1919 through the 1920s the pace of life and technology quickened. Ross and Keith Smith took up a challenge from the government and flew from Britain to Australia in 27 days 20 hours in a twin-engined Vickers Vimy arriving in Darwin at 3 p.m. on 10 December 1919. In 1920 Qantas (Queensland and Northern Territory Aerial Service) was formed by Hudson Fysh, Fergus McMaster and Paul McGuiness. By November 1920 Qantas was operating out of Winton, Queensland with a paid up capital of £100 000 and two Avro 504K biplanes.

In 1921 the Second Commonwealth Census revealed that the full-blood aboriginal population had dropped to 60 000, further illustrating the neglect with which Australians had treated the indigenous population.

Dee Why Beach, Sydney in about 1939.

Radio broadcasting began in 1923 with the establishment of 2SB in Sydney. Rich deposits of silver-lead-zinc ore were discovered in north-west Queensland and the leases were named Mount Isa. Construction of the first Parliament House in Canberra began in the same year along with the commencement of construction of the Sydney Harbour Bridge.

The next few years saw the end of Cobb & Co., the opening of Woolworths stores, the beginning of the forty-four hour working week, the continuation of assisted immigration from Britain, the establishment of the CSIRO, the eradication of the prickly pear infestation and in 1927 Canberra became the seat of Federal Government.

Aviation continued to dazzle the population. In 1928 Bert Hinkler made the first solo flight from Britain to Australia in fifteen and one half days slashing Ross and Keith Smith's record by nearly fifty per cent and in the same year Sir Charles Kingsford Smith and Charles Ulm made the first trans-Pacific Flight from California to Brisbane, Queensland. Qantas inaugurated Australia's first daily air service in Queensland between Brisbane and Toowoomba and the Flying Doctor Service officially commenced operation. On a less optimistic note thirty-two aborigines were killed by whites in retaliation for an Aboriginal attack on a station holder and the killing of a white dingo shooter.

In 1930 Donald Bradman made 334 runs in a Test match against England at Leeds and Phar Lap entered his second Melbourne Cup Race as favourite and, ridden by Jim Pike, won by 3 lengths. But in the same year Australians began to experience the effects of the worldwide depression—businesses were failing and 20 per cent of workers were unemployed. The horrific effects of the depression continued for the next three years. Unemployment peaked in 1933 at 30 percent. The harsh face of the depression was seen in the horrendous size of the dole queues, the sudden appearance of shanty towns, tough economic measures, declining living standards and immense hardships. Australia was reeling from the impact of dramatically declining commodity prices and mounting overseas debt. In April 1931 the collapse of the New South Wales State Savings Bank appeared imminent and after a rush of depositors, it was forced to close its doors. To add to the sadness of the times Phar Lap died in the USA and murmours of poisoning appeared in the press. It was to be the year 2000 before these suspicions were finally put to rest by modern research procedures.

Economic conditions gradually improved and events such as the opening of the Sydney Harbour Bridge and the controversial 'bodyline' cricket series momentarily took the public's mind off the daily hardships of the period.

Kylie Tennant's first novel *Tiburon* and Christina Stead's *Seven Poor Men of Sydney* were published in 1935. Ernestine Hill's *The Great Australian Loneliness* was published in 1937 and Xavier Herbert's *Capricornia* in 1938. The *Dad and Dave* serial entertained radio listeners and aboriginal water colourist Albert Namitjira held his first public exhibition in Melbourne in 1938. In the same year the 150th Anniversary of Phillip's landing at Sydney Cove was celebrated and re-enacted at Botany Bay. But developments in Europe were bringing grim forebodings of further difficult times ahead.

World War II and postwar prosperity

On 3 September 1939 the then Prime Minister Robert Menzies went on radio to announce:

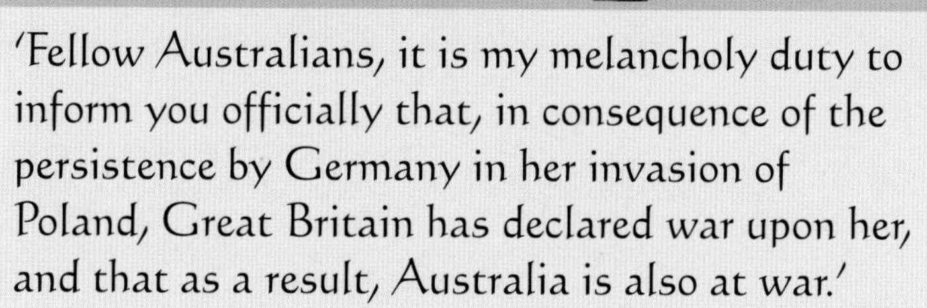

'Fellow Australians, it is my melancholy duty to inform you officially that, in consequence of the persistence by Germany in her invasion of Poland, Great Britain has declared war upon her, and that as a result, Australia is also at war.'

The nation's passion for war and the belief that it was nation-building and character-building was clear. People queued to join the forces and the newspapers wrote eulogies about the brave men who were going off to fight for their country.

The *Sydney Morning Herald* described the departure of six thousand soldiers from Sydney on 5 January 1940:

> Six thousand young soldiers of the Second A.I.F., proud bearers of the standard bequeathed to them by the original Anzacs, marched through the streets of the city yesterday. A tumultuous reception was given them by dense crowds, estimated to number nearly 500,000.
>
> The long khaki columns thrilled the heart of Sydney as it has not been thrilled for a quarter of a century, since that still spring day in 1914 when the First A.I.F. marched through the same streets on its way to Anzac and imperishable glory.
>
> These men of Australia's brave new army, young, bronzed, clear-eyed, and so obviously conscious in their demeanour of their high responsibility and the confidence which a nation reposes in them, were the answer to Berlin's wishful propaganda. They were worth, in terms of patriotic showmanship, ten times all the supply ships and the food ships which Australia has sent to the European war zone since the war began...

By the beginning of 1940 Australia's over-seas 'obligations' were clear. That year was notable for its preparations to defend Australia against possible invasion: a Volunteer Defence Corps was established; Bass Strait was closed to shipping after a British ship hit a mine; and the first of many rationing measures—petrol rationing—was introduced.

Perhaps the most significant moment of World War II (as far as Australia was concerned) occurred in 1942 when Japan entered the war and started its push south which, by the end of the year, would see the first attacks on Australian soil since European settlement.

The year before (1941) had seen the Australian Government suffer a crisis of confidence, the ruling coalition collapse, and Robert Menzies resign as Prime Minister. In his wake came John Curtin, and it was Curtin's hapless duty to announce the nation's greatest naval disaster as 645 servicemen died when HMAS *Sydney* was destroyed by the Germans off the coast of Western Australia.

In 1942, for the first time in history, foreign invaders killed civilian Australians on Australian soil (243 died in Darwin as a result of Japanese air raids). It was the year when the Australian towns of Broome and Wyndham were bombed, and when three midget Japanese suicide submarines broke through the safety net and attacked shipping in Sydney Harbour.

Rationing was intensified as the demands of the war ate deeper into the healthiness of the Australian economy. By 1943 there were restrictions on the sale of cooking appliances and rationing of household drapery.

By 1943 the Japanese were on the retreat. In that year too, Darwin saw the last bombing raid after some fifty-nine attacks. Signs that the war was drawing to a close were apparent as work was completed on Hobart's famous floating bridge across the Derwent and in Western Australia the Australian National Airways was established.

Although the war did not finish until 1945, the major events of 1944—with the obvious exceptions of the introduction of meat rationing and the Japanese prisoner-of-war breakout of Cowra (which resulted in the deaths of 232 prisoners)—were domestic issues. The country was racked by natural disasters with bush-fires in Victoria claiming fifty-one lives and the worst dust storms on record sweeping across south-eastern Australia.

R. G. (later Sir Robert) Menzies.

In 1945, just a month before the end of the war, John Curtin died in office. He was succeeded for just five days by Francis Forde before Ben Chifley, 'a true product of the Australian Labor movement' (as *The Times* in London described him), became Prime Minister.

The postwar years were characterised by demobilisation, immigration and reconstruction. As Minister for Immigration, Arthur Calwell instituted a huge drive for European migrants which, by the late 1950s, had brought more than a million Greeks and Italians, and substantial numbers of Dutch, Yugoslavs, English and Spaniards to Australia. The program was rationalised as humanitarian aid to a war-torn Europe but it was also driven by a fear of imminent invasion from the north—a fear which had proved to be a reality during 1942 and 1943.

Reconstruction and recovery saw the establishment of Trans Australian Airlines, the development of Woomera as an experimental site and the opening of the Australian National University (ANU); Qantas was nationalised and an Antarctic survey station was built on Heard Island.

In 1946 cars finally outnumbered horses and thus became the country's main mode of transport. This fact was neatly reinforced two years later when, on 29 November 1948, Prime Minister Ben Chifley stood at the end of a production line at Fisherman's Bend and watched the first Holden 48/215 (the first 'Australian' car) come off the assembly line. For Chifley it fulfilled his dream of a low cost, hardy, people's car. It cost £733 10s and by 1951 General Motors-Holden's (GMH) were producing over a hundred vehicles a day.

The recovery from the Great Depression and World War II was complete and people settled back into a comfortable society where thoughts of war and strife were pushed to the back of their minds.

Towards an Australian identity—A decade of change

Major cultural changes are usually the product of complex and subtle factors which occur slowly and are often hard to identify. In recent times Australians have started to discuss the possibility of becoming a republic, have seen the need for reconciliation with Aborigines, and the importance of focussing the country's industrial activity more towards the buoyant economies of Asia.

It is hard to account for the winds which swept through Australian political life in the decade between 1965 and 1975. Why should we change? The postwar years had been good to Australia. The government led by Robert (later Sir Robert) Menzies had ruled over the country benignly and most people were satisfied There had been little or no unemployment. Large projects like the Snowy Mountains Hydro-Electricity Scheme and the Murrumbidgee Irrigation Scheme had started. England was 'home' and Queen Elizabeth II was loved and admired. Australia may not have been very exciting but it was very comfortable.

Building the Sydney Opera House continues through 1966.

As much as any generalisation has validity it would seem that the defining force of change in the mid-1960s was the sudden explosion of young adults known as 'the baby boomers'. A new word, 'teenager', entered the language. The conservative forces—education, the law, parents, social morality—were being challenged by a phalanx of youth whose catch-cry was 'The times they are a'changin'. Movies like *Blackboard Jungle* and *The Wild One*, actors like James Dean and Marlon Brando, musicians and singers like Elvis Presley and Jerry Lee Lewis, had given notice in the 1950s that change was in the air.

In the 1960s, there was an even more potent force at work. The pre-eminent cultural force was popular music. Singers and groups like Bob Dylan, The Beatles and the Rolling Stones not only provided the soundtrack but they also provided the hairstyles, clothes, recreational activities, and the political focus.

In Australia an era symbolically ended when Sir Robert Menzies retired on 20 January 1966. It was as though, at that moment, the easy postwar security and conservatism was over. Already Australia was embroiled in Vietnam and the first baby boomers were old enough to vote.

The unfortunate Harold Holt tried to maintain the status quo but events were beyond his control. He could proudly declare that he was 'All the way with LBJ' but Lyndon Baines Johnson would retreat from office under a welter of anti-Vietnam rallies and protests.

The tide of world events had been running against the Liberal Party. The moral and economic conservatism and the allegiance to Britain and the United States which had been the cornerstone of the Menzies years were coming under attack. Australian jingoism was being replaced by an informed nationalism. The commitment in Vietnam was under attack in both the United States and Australia. The 'swinging sixties' with their new liberalism and sexual freedom were chal-

Sydney's Warringah Expressway approach to the Harbour Bridge under construction in 1966.

Melbourne's Westgate Bridge almost completed in 1976.

lenging the morality of the early postwar years.

It was an accident of history which jettisoned John Gorton into this period of flux. When Harold Holt drowned at Cheviot Beach near Portsea on 17 December 1967 the Liberal Party was thrown into chaos.

The contenders for the prime ministership included Senator John Gorton, Leslie Bury, Billy Snedden and Deputy Leader William McMahon. McMahon was eliminated when John McEwan, Leader of the Country Party, threatened to break the coalition if he won the leadership ballot. All the other candidates seemed lacklustre.

To the surprise of many, John Gorton won. Thus, on 10 January 1968, he became the first senator to be elected Prime Minister, although shortly afterwards he moved to the House of Representatives, having won Harold Holt's seat in a by-election.

Gorton caught the mood of the times. He challenged the stuffy formality of the Liberal Party and his brief prime ministership (he voted himself out the office on 10 March 1971) was characterised by a liberalism and commitment to change which anticipated the Whitlam era.

Gorton is a near-perfect example of John Kenneth Galbraith's argument that history is driven by the necessity of events not the ideology of individuals. Although he was a conservative he was driven by the mood of the times. During his brief period in office he saw changes in Australian society which included the creation of the Australian Council for the Arts, the completion and opening of the National Library of Australia, the establishment of the liberal–conservative Australia Party, the introduction of the concept of equal pay for women, an agreement to establish Australia's first legal gambling casino at Wrest Point near Hobart, the creation of the Metric Conversion Board, the liberalising of abortion laws in South Australia, the first Aborigine to enter Federal Parliament and Aborigines included in the national census.

In many ways, 1971 was a watershed year for Aborigines. It was a year when the changing attitudes in Australian society began to have an impact on the rights of Aborigines. Still, in a very real sense, victories were tempered by setbacks.

The fight for land rights, which was to dominate Aboriginal thinking throughout the 1970s and 1980s, saw both victories and defeats. In January the Victorian Government of Sir Henry Bolte announced that the Aboriginal reserves at Lake Tyers in the Gippsland region and around Framlington would be handed over to the local Aboriginal communities. However, in April the people of Yirrkala lost their land rights battle in the Northern Territory Supreme Court.

In May 1971, when a casual Senate vacancy occurred in Queensland, Neville Bonner became the first Aborigine to take a seat in the Federal Parliament. Although he was hardly a radical, Bonner did attempt to champion the Aboriginal cause.

Then, on 30 June, for the first time since 1901, full-blooded Aborigines were included in a Federal Census. Against this background C. D. Rowley's *The Destruction of Aboriginal Society* was published. It was the first major acknowledgment by white society that white settlement in Australia had been the cause of the decimation of the Aboriginal people.

In hindsight it has been common to attribute these changes to Gough Whitlam and the ALP. The fact was that the mood of the late 1960s

could not be denied by any politician. Perhaps the only difference between Gorton and Whitlam was that Gorton was caught up and swept along by events while Whitlam, sniffing the changes, embraced them with enthusiasm.

In 1971, after a party room vote of confidence which resulted in a tie, John Gorton, who had the casting vote, voted himself out of office and William McMahon came to power. But, by now, the ALP juggernaut was unstoppable.

On 13 November 1972 Gough Whitlam, Leader of the Federal ALP, opened the party's election campaign at Blacktown Civic Centre with the famous lines:

> Men and women of Australia, the decision we will make for our country on 2 December is a choice between the past and the future, between the habits and fears of the past and the demands and opportunities of the future. There are moments in history when the whole fate and future of nations can be decided by a single decision. For Australia, this is such a time.

After twenty-three years of Liberal government the Australian electorate was being asked to choose between a party which had been ruled by four leaders—Menzies, Holt, Gorton and McMahon—in six years and a party which had been dominated by Gough Whitlam since 1966.

The Labor campaign, with the slogan 'It's Time' and a catchy pop song accompanying its television commercials, caught the popular imagination. When the election was held on 2 December Whitlam achieved 49.6 per cent of the vote, giving him a nine-seat majority.

Whitlam was a man in a hurry. He could not wait for the formal establishment of a new ministry. For three weeks he ran the country with his Deputy Prime Minister, Lance Barnard. This two-man ministry controlled twenty-seven portfolios. In three weeks they set out to wipe away the detritus of twenty-three years of Liberal government. They repealed the Conscription Act, released National Service protesters from gaol, looked into the issue of equal pay for women, banned sporting teams from Rhodesia (now Zimbabwe) and South Africa, set up an inquiry into Aboriginal land rights, withdrew troops from Vietnam, and investigated grants to public and private schools.

On 18 December a full ministry was chosen. Again the pace of legislation was rapid and by the end of 1972 the Whitlam government's popularity had soared. The public perception was that here was a government which was going to improve both Australian society and the well-being of individuals within that society.

The Brisbane city skyline in 1979.

In October 1986 the Royal Australian Navy held their 75th Anniversary celebrations on Sydney Harbour. HRH the Duke of Edinburgh is on board the white ship HMAS *Cook* taking the salute.

The end result was the Whitlam government changed Australian society irrevocably. Although, on balance, he was an unsuccessful Prime Minister, his vision of a new, liberal, adventurous society was to persist. It still permeates Australian thinking today.

The emergence of modern Australia

Edward Gough Whitlam may have been a man in a hurry but he was also a Prime Minister with a vision of a new, more independent and self-confident Australia.

There are thousands of vantage points for looking at the way societies change. Each has its own merits. One image that seems to sum up the changes of the 1970s is the way the book publishing industry began to view the 'Australiana' market.

In 1971 if you wanted a large, glossy book with lots of good photographs of Australia you bought *The Australians* (text by George Johnson, photographs by Robert B. Goodman). It had been first published in 1966 and in the following five years it seemed as though every home had a copy.

By 1981 whole sections of bookshops had been given over to 'Australiana'. Huge books, commonly with a photograph of what was then called 'Ayers Rock' on the cover, were piled on shelves which sagged under their weight. From a point of indifference we had become a nation eager to devour everything about the country.

Somewhere in the 1970s Australia became very proud of its uniqueness and identity. This process probably reached its apotheosis in 1988 when the bicentennial was celebrated with an orgy of self-congratulation and pride.

There are moments throughout the 1970s and 1980s which still loom large in the nation's consciousness. These are moments when pride in country felt good and when we seemed to be capable of matching the achievements of any other society. There are also moments when Australians asserted their independence from the historic control of Britain and the United States.

If, for example, the anti-Vietnam rallies of 1970 challenged the relationship Australia had with the United States then so too did the

Proclamation of Australia Act which was signed by Queen Elizabeth in Canberra in 1986 and which finally broke the legal ties between Australia and Britain. In themselves these two acts seem small but in the way that they defined a new feeling of independence they were significant. On 8 May 1970 an estimated 200 000 people marched in the streets of Australia's capital cities to protest about Australian involvement in Vietnam. This wasn't just student radicalism it was a spontaneous outpouring of a belief that Australia could make decision without being cajoled into them by larger powers.

Similarly the final cutting of the legal umbilical cord between Britain and Australia which started in 1982 when the High Court became the final court of appeal and appeals to the British Privy Council were stopped was also a change in mood. Again it was Australia saying that it could sort out its own problems. There was no need to be dependent on Britain for legal decisions.

On a more superficial level the assertion of Australianness manifested itself in enormous public gatherings and celebrations. The official opening of the Sydney Opera House in 1973 saw a huge fireworks display and the lighting up of the harbour. Again this kind of celebration would be repeated over and over again in the coming years. In 1988 it was estimated that two million people lined the shores of the harbour on 26 January to celebrate the Bicentennial and once again to watch fireworks and extravagant displays on the harbour. Similarly the outpouring of joy when Sydney won the right to host the 2000 Olympics again saw the harbour lit up and huge celebrations on the shore. Even this event paled into insignificance when compared to the magnificent pyrotechnic dispays conducted at the opening and closing ceremonies of the enormously successful Olympic Games in 2000. These were all acts of pride. People were gathering to declare a love of country and a commitment to the nation.

Australia's Aussat I communications satellite is launched from the space shuttle Discovery on 31 August 1985.

Behind these public displays were the more subtle changes. The arts, which had never enjoyed a huge profile, came to prominence during the Whitlam era when in 1973 Patrick White became the first Australian to win the Nobel Prize for Literature. That same year the Australian National Gallery purchased Jackson Pollock's Blue Poles for $1.3 million amid considerable public debate. But the quiet artistic achiever was the Australian film industry.

Starting tentatively with a series of superbly filmed historic dramas—*Picnic At Hanging Rock* (Russell Boyd won a British Academy Award for the Best Photography), *The Getting of Wisdom, Sunday Too Far Away, Newsfront* and *My Brilliant Career*—the 1970s ended with the industry making commercial movies which were enjoying huge success in international markets.

The change occurred at the end of the decade when *Mad Max* became Australia's most successful international film ever. Through the 1980s it was followed by such acclaimed and successful movies as *'Breaker' Morant, Gallipoli, Mad Max 2, The Year of Living Dangerously, Bliss, Mad Max: Beyond Thunderdome, Crocodile Dundee, Crocodile Dundee II, Evil Angels, Young Einstein, Dead Calm* and, in the 1990s, movies like *Strictly Ballroom, The Piano, Ferngully: The Last Rainforest, Priscilla, Queen of the Desert* and *Muriel's Wedding*.

The arts may have gloried in their successes but the sense of sporting achievement was equally significant and defining. In the 1950s Australians had been naturally good sportspeople. The nation's swimmers, tennis players, footballers and cricketers were the best in the world but they were all enthusiastic amateurs. As sport took on a more rigorous, more professional complexion Australian athletes found that they could not match the expertise of highly paid, full-time sportspeople.

This change in the nature of Australian sport occurred with the establishment of the government-funded Australian Institute of Sport. The AIS's most obvious early success was Robert de Castella who, in 1981, joined the organisation as a sports biophysicist and went on to become one of the finest marathon runners of his generation.

In the world of commercial sport the highlights of the era included Pat Cash's win at Wimbledon in 1983, the holding of the first Australian Grand Prix motor race in Adelaide in 1985 and, looming large over the 1980s, the America's Cup victory of Alan Bond's winged-keeled yacht *Australia II*, which had been designed by Ben Lexcen and skippered by John Bertrand. After twenty-one years of trying to win the elusive cup it was a victory that seemed to capture the mood of optimism which existed in the country in 1983.

Almost forgotten in this hub-bub of success were the smaller events which were symbolic of a more confident, more relaxed nation. In 1976 the liberal-minded and progressive Premier of South Australia, Don Dunstan, achieved a significant breakthrough when he appointed Pastor Sir Douglas Nicholls Governor of South Australia. It was a symbolic gesture. Nicholls became Australia's first Aboriginal State Governor.

Equally, the decision to grant leasehold title to the Gurundji people in 1975 was the beginning of a process which would culminate in the admission that land had been taken from Aborigines. The historic Mabo decision would attempt to redress this perception of unfairness.

This was also a time when Australia finally embraced the concept of a universal health insurance system, changed its national anthem, and looked toward the future with a sense of optimism and genuine enthusiasm. It seemed as though the country had achieved a sense of independence and nationhood which had been accepted broadly by the majority of citizens

Towards reconciliation

(by Dalys Newman)

In the last three decades of the twentieth century, there has been significant development in the rights of Aboriginal people. As Aborigines have become more determined and whites more socially

conscious, many errors of the past are being redressed.

In 1972 the Whitlam government introduced a policy of self-determination, which recognised the rights of Aboriginal people to live traditional life-styles if they wished to do so. The Federal Department of Aboriginal Affairs was established, and Justice A.E. Woodward was appointed to head a Royal Commission into the issue of Aboriginal land rights in the Northern Territory. The Woodward Report recommended that all Aboriginal reserve lands be returned to the Aboriginal inhabitants and that other Crown land be returned to the local Aborigines if they could prove traditional claims to it. These recommendations were put into effect in the Aboriginal Land Rights Act of 1976.

In 1981 the South Australian government handed the Pitjantjatjara lands back to their traditional owners, and in 1983, the New South Wales Aboriginal Land Rights Act began a process by which the state government could buy back land for Aboriginal groups. In 1985, Uluru (Ayers Rock) was handed back to its Aboriginal owners in the Northern Territory.

In 1989, the Aboriginal and Torres Strait Islander Commission (ATSIC), a powerful Aboriginal body, was established. It administerd a government-funded billion dollar budget and coordinated 60 regional councils. This body was empowered to provide grants for projects in Aboriginal health, recreation, justice, community infrastructure, heritage, arts, culture, communication, housing and business. In 1991 the Hawke government established a Council for Aboriginal Reconciliation whose vision statement was: 'A united Australia which respects this land of ours; values the Aboriginal and Torres Strait Islander heritage; and provides justice and equity for all.'

The most significant and controversial change was introduced by the High Court in 1992 in a finding now known as 'Mabo'. In this victory for indigenous land rights, the Court ruled in favour of a writ issued by Torres Strait Islander, Eddie Mabo, claiming that his people, inhabitants of the Murray Islands, owned land on the islands because they had lived there since 'time immemorial'. The Mabo decision ruled that the Murray Islanders held native title over their land in spite of the arrival of Europeans. This finding meant that the indigenous Australians were the original owners of the land, thus paving the way for similar claims elsewhere. Mabo destroyed forever the legal concept that Australia was *terra nullius*, an empty land, before the arrival of Europeans. In the Mabo decision, Justice Brennan wrote: 'Where a clan or group has continued to acknowledge the laws and to observe the customs based on the traditions of that clan or group whereby their traditional connection with the land has been substantially maintained, the traditional community title of that clan or group can be said to remain in existence.'

In 1994, Prime Minister Paul Keating gave the Mabo decision legislative teeth with the Native Title Act, which established tribunals to decide which lands should be returned to Aboriginal claimants. The government announced $1.46 billion over 10 years for a national land fund to be used for the purchase and management of land and housing.

The first case to come before the High Court under the new Act was brought by the Wik people of Queensland, who claimed native title rights to land that was under pastoral lease. The Court found that the existence of a pastoral lease did not extinguish any Aboriginal right to the same land—such title could co-exist. This ruling increased the scope for Aboriginal claims and created economic uncertainty for pastoralists, who began to clamour for blanket extinguishment of native title. In 1997, the Howard government, in an effort to clarify ambiguities and produce a more workable system for claims introduced a Ten-Point Plan, which was passed by the Senate in July 1998.

To process land claims, the Act provided for tribunals to be established within each state by the respective governments. The administration of Native Title and compensation policies will continue to be a significant issue in the future.

Despite considerable advances in relation to the treatment of the Aboriginal people, the process of reconciliation has been hampered by various recent issues including: the Howard government's refusal to apologise for the stolen generation, threats of Aboriginal activism during the Olympic Games and the ongoing problem of Aboriginal deaths in custody.

During the early years of the twenty-first there was much controversy about the leadership of ATSIC. In response to this in March 2004 new Labor leader Mark Latham promised to abolish the Commission if Labor came to power. On 15 April 2004 the Prime Minister, John Howard announced his government's decision to abolish ATSIC immediately.

Australia Today (by Dalys Newman)

Having reached a population of 20 million, in 2003, Australia is entering the twenty-first century with independence and dynamism. The outstanding success of the staging of the Sydney Olympics in 2000 was a fitting climax to a century of incredible growth.

Since the turn of the century, Australia finds itself enjoying a bouyant economy and a continuing up-ward rate of growth. Unemployment has reached a much lower level than those of the 1990s, and experts agree that growth will be sustainable in the medium-term future.

The tragic Bali bombing, made Australians aware of our vulnerability in a changing world and the country's involvement in the wars in Afghanistan and Iraq, though very controversial, has certainly heightened Australia's profile in most parts of the world.

The Australian people are basically content with their lot and the country continues to be a vibrant and important democracy in a rapidly developing part of the world.

Looking towards the future (by Bruce Elder)

At the beginning of the twenty-first century, Australian society has been nudged towards a need to redefine itself. Australia's position in the world, despite a hugely successful 'best ever' Olympic Games, is less certain than a decade ago. The push to become part of Asia is now seen as possibly an error of judgement. The world perceives the country as a European society with an old economy based on mining and commodities and has valued the Australian dollar accordingly even though much has been done in the information technology areas. There's no doubt that Australians will rise to the challenges of the twenty-first century, just as they have in past crises. And this 'rising to the challenges' applies not only to times of crisis but also seems to pervade the thinking of the people in times of great events such as the recent Olympics and Paralympics. Here the country clearly showed the world just how tolerant and enthusiastic its people can become and how the country can work together to celebrate the differences in a positive way. It is this tolerance and enthusiasm which will ultimately win through and true reconciliation with our indigenous people will become a splendid reality. With so much of our culture built upon the indigenous people and the new arrivals from all over the world the country is well placed to achieve. The old image of a predominantly Anglo-Saxon outpost of the British Empire is gone. The country has genuinely become multicultural and multinational. Inevitably there has been racial friction but it has, by the standards of other countries with large immigration programs, been low level and rarely seriously violent.

The Australia of the 1950s was a society where tea and beer were the most popular adult drinks, where restaurants offered lamb or beef 'with two veg', where men wore grey suits and ties and women wore furs, pearls and 'sensible' clothes and where cheddar cheese, brawn and devon were the high points of the local delicatessen and where brown bread was considered a bit daring. It was a deeply conservative society emotionally tied to Britain which, in the minds of many, was referred to as 'home' and 'the mother country'.

The Union Jack was flown higher than the Australian flag at important occasions, 'God Save the Queen' was Australia's national anthem and images of a youthful Queen Elizabeth II were neatly framed on a wall in every public building.

In forty years the country has changed dramatically. Wine, boutique beers and endless Mediterranean variations of coffee have overwhelmed beer and tea. Urban centres offer a bewildering variety of cuisines ranging from American fast food through Vietnamese, Thai, Indian, Spanish and Mexican to African and South American. Suits and furs have given way to casual attire, multicoloured elegance and, for young people, the persuasiveness of designer labels.

Delicatessens are bewildering storehouses of international meats and cheeses and exotic delicacies. The conservatism of the 1950s has given way to a society eager to embrace change—Australians have purchased electronic toys with extraordinary enthusiasm—and eager to be seen as part of the international community.

It is easy to see these changes as cosmetic. In fact they are symbolic of deeper changes in the nature of Australian society. These changes can be summarised as a belief that Australia needs to define itself according to its future rather than its past. Thus, a society which once actively discouraged migration from Asia now recognises that its future is inextricably linked with the rapidly developing economies of south-east Asia and the Pacific rim.

A society where once Latin and French were the most popular languages taught in schools now focusses its language education programs on Japanese and Indonesian. A society which traditionally relied on its primary production—particularly wool, wheat, meat and mining products—for its economic prosperity now declares that its future lies in becoming a 'clever country'.

The vision for the future is rich and complex. It can be summed up as a combination of a need for national identity, a need to find a realistic place in an increasingly complex modern world, and a need to take our place alongside the great, independent nations of the world.

Australians have been talking about a sense of national identity for most of the twentieth century. In the years immediately prior to federation the *Bulletin*, and writers like Henry Lawson, had championed the notion that a fiercely independent, hard-working and resilient rural worker was the true Australian. It was an image which mixed the courage of the Eureka Stockade, the tenacity of The Drover's Wife, the anti-authority feelings of the early convicts, with liberal doses of drought, dust, flies and hardship and added pain and suffering for good measure.

This image seemed to become a reality during World War I. When the image of Australian soldiers on the battlefield connected with the image of the resilient rural worker. This image, subsequently made more potent by actors like 'Snowy' Baker and Chips Rafferty, persisted until the 1980s. It may well be the case that Bryan Brown and Bob Hawke, particularly the latter in his 'larrikin' mode, were the last hurrahs of this image.

Australians of the future will be distanced from any notion of England as 'home'. They will acknowledge that the Europeanisation of Australia was a result of British colonial expansionism in the late eighteenth century and will admit that there was once a society which looked to Britain for its political and legal institutions. These new Australians will acknowledge that Australian Aborigines were forcibly dispossessed of their land, and will rejoice in the sense that modern Australia is a melting pot of cultures where people enjoy the benefits of older cultures while not being tied to the superiority of those cultures.

In many ways such an image of Australia is a dream. However, the changes which have occurred in Australia in the past twenty years do suggest quite plainly that the old order will never return and that as Australia makes its way forward in the twenty-first century it will hold its head high in the world community of nations. It will rejoice in its independence and its dynamism.

Sydney Harbour from Shark Point in the 1880s.

The Gap, near South Head, Sydney

The flag of New South Wales (the first state).
This flag was adopted on 18 February 1876 and is basically a British Blue Ensign with the state badge sitting on a blue background. The badge is a cross of St George in red on a white disc. An eight pointed gold star sits at the end of each arm of the cross with a passant guardant lion situated in the centre. The badge was designed by James Barnet, the Colonial Architect and a retired naval officer, Captain Francis Hixson.

New South Wales has adopted the Waratah as its floral emblem, the kookaburra as its faunal emblem, the platypus as its animal emblem and the blue groper as its marine emblem.

New South Wales: The Heritage

by Bruce Elder

In the beginning, New South Wales was the name applied to more than half of the Australian continent. Captain James Cook, having sailed up the eastern coastline of Australia stood on Possession Island at the tip of Cape York on 22 August 1770 and claimed the entire eastern coastline of Australia in the name of King George III, the reigning British monarch. It was, as history has shown, an extraordinary act. All the way up the coast Cook had seen the fires from Aboriginal camps and at numerous places he had sighted Aborigines on beaches and headlands and yet, in spite of British regulations regarding inhabited lands, he claimed the east coast as though it had no human habitation. By doing so he set in motion the forces which, fifteen years later, would result in England establishing a penal colony at Port Jackson.

When Cook claimed the east coast he did not name it. Evidence shows that the name 'New South Wales' came to him on the homeward journey and he recorded it in his journal.

The decision to create a penal colony in this far-flung land was the result of forces which created a serious shortage of facilities for convicts in Britain in the late eighteenth century and after the American War of Independence North America could no longer be used for this purpose. Equally the Industrial Revolution saw people pouring into the larger cities and consequently the crime rate in London had risen to a point where it could not be handled by the prisons in Britain.

In 1786 the British parliament decided that Botany Bay would be a suitable penal colony and so, on 13 May 1787, a fleet of eleven ships carrying convicts and marines set sail from Portsmouth bound for New South Wales. They reached their destination on 18 January 1788 but it became immediately obvious that the lack of fresh water would ensure the failure of the colony. Governor Arthur Phillip, who was in charge of the settlement, sent an exploration party north where, only a few kilometres up the coast, they entered Port Jackson. In Phillip's assessment it was 'the finest harbour in the world, in which a thousand sail of the line might ride in perfect security'. It also had reliable fresh water.

Thus, on 26 January 1788 Phillip raised the Union Jack in Sydney Cove and the colony of New South Wales was formally established. The early life was hard. The settlement started with nothing. Houses had to be built, streets and lanes carved out of the slopes on either side of the Tank Stream, quarters constructed for the soldiers and convicts, fields planted, animals grazed and the countryside explored. This was the true origin of New South Wales. A dirty and desolate penal colony at the end of the world.

The Argyle Cut, Sydney in the 1880s.

The first years in the colony were very difficult. The supplies which had been brought on the First Fleet were inadequate. The tools were unsuitable and the expertise of both the convicts and the soldiers was limited. The colony waited for every new ship from England, Batavia and the Cape of Good Hope. When a ship did not arrive the colony was on the edge of starvation.

The rapid development of the colony was driven by necessity rather than some adventurous management program. By 1791 land had been granted to over 150 people in the hope that the agricultural base of the infant settlement could be broadened. The problem was still one of expertise and Phillip eventually pleaded with the British government to send out free settlers with farming experience so New South Wales could become self-sufficient. This call was answered and by the mid-1790s farms, with convicts as the workers, were providing Sydney with supplies.

Given that he had started with a beach and no water and had, in the space of four years, found water, settled the land and made it productive, it is important that Arthur Phillip is recognised as the true father of New South Wales. It was his tenacity and determination which converted Sydney into a viable colony and set the base upon which New South Wales, the most populous of the Australian states, was created.

In the years that followed a series of Governors, most of them with military or naval backgrounds, battled to solve the problems of the new colony. In order, the governors were: Major Francis Grose (1792–94), Captain William Paterson (1794–95), Captain John Hunter, RN (1794–1800), Captain Philip Gidley King, RN (1800–06), Captain William Bligh, RN (1806–08), Lieutenant-Colonel George Johnston (1808), Lieutenant-Colonel Joseph Foveaux (1808–09), and Colonel William Paterson (1809). Some achieved fame and notoriety. King, for example, was responsible for extensive coastal exploration and was the governor who granted John Macarthur land (which led to the establishment of the very lucrative market in fine wool); and Bligh, already the victim of a mutiny, was publicly humiliated and forced to leave the colony after he attempted to control the power of the military.

At this time all of the east coast and hinterland was part of New South Wales and so the exploration of the coast which ranged from the discovery of the Hunter and Hawkesbury rivers in the north to the circumnavigation of Van Diemen's Land, was all considered part of the larger exploration of New South Wales.

The great challenge, however, lay inland from Sydney. The Blue Mountains seemed impassible to the explorers who made their way across the Sydney basin. When, after numerous attempts, they were finally crossed in 1813 by the explorers Blaxland, Wentworth and Lawson, it was merely a question of the time before the whole of New South Wales was settled.

It is appropriate that this major exploration milestone was reached during the governorship of Lachlan Macquarie. Macquarie, who was Governor from 1810 to 1823, transformed the struggling

colony into a thriving and successful region.

During his administration numerous public buildings were constructed with the help of the gifted ex-convict Francis Greenaway, education and the treatment of women and children was addressed, the first bank (the Bank of New South Wales) was granted a charter, and exploration and settlement proceeded at a dramatic pace. By the time Macquarie returned to England the colony had been explored from Port Macquarie in the north to the Lachlan and Macquarie rivers in the west and Jervis Bay in the south.

Fort Macquarie (where the Sydney Opera House now stands) in the 1880s.

In 1823 Macquarie established the basis for the state's Legislative Council. It was the first move towards some kind of self government. That same year the Supreme Court was given full independence and the old military rule (which had existed since 1788) began to be phased out.

The history of New South Wales from 1825 until the 1860s is that of a colony which kept shrinking due to the establishment of independent new colonies. In 1825 Van Diemen's Land was separated. This was followed in 1851 by Victoria and 1859 by Queensland. In each case the development of a community with interests which were different from those emanating from Sydney resulted in new colonies being given some measure of autonomy.

During this period the penal nature of the colony was replaced by a society where free settlers and emancipated convicts worked together.

As the population increased the needs of New South Wales changed. During Major-General Ralph Darling's governorship (1825–31) the colony's Legislative Council was enlarged and government customs offices, postal services and a land office were all created.

The colony's focus on agriculture during this period resulted in a population of 2.75 million sheep in 1838. By the 1840s explorers like Sir Thomas Mitchell and others reached the Darling Downs (now in southern Queensland), Portland Bay (Victoria) and the Murray River (South Australia). They were quickly followed by squatters and settlers who claimed the land as soon as it was explored.

The great turning point in the state's history occurred in the area around Bathurst and Orange on 12 February 1851 when Edward Hargraves and a colleague, John Lister, successfully panned gold. In May 1851 Hargraves took 120 grams of gold to Sydney and showed it to the Colonial Secretary and on 14 May the gold discovery was announced.

The impact of this event sent shock waves through all the Australian colonies and changed the nature of Australian society. Over night, workers in Sydney downed tools and headed for the goldfields. Miners and prospectors from all over the world arrived in Sydney eager to get to the goldfields and try their luck.

It was now clear that the old administrative mechanisms which had kept New South Wales tied to the British parliament were irrelevant. The British handed over control of land policy to the NSW Legislative Council in 1852 and a form of responsible government was granted when, in 1855,

an elected lower house, the Legislative Assembly, was created.

In the decade from 1851 to 1861 the population of the New South Wales nearly doubled—from 197 000 to 350 000. The rural squattocracy which had traditionally controlled the state were now in a minority but, because of the unfairness of the electoral system, they still controlled both houses of parliament.

The state continued to expand throughout the 1870s and 1880s. Railways were built across the Blue Mountains and the combination of Cobb & Co. coaches, bullock wagons (which had to travel on rough bush tracks) and railway lines, opened up the state. The prosperity of the agricultural sector of the state's economy in the last years of the nineteenth century ensured a lasting and strong economic base.

The period leading up to the outbreak of World War I was a boom time for New South Wales. The area of the state under wheat, greatly helped by the Federation strain of the grain developed by William Farrer, grew to a massive 1.4 million hectares. Rural credit was readily available to farmers wishing to expand. The advent of refrigeration opened up overseas and interstate markets. Mining of silver-lead at Broken Hill and coal in the Hunter Valley expanded rapidly.

The outbreak of World War I fuelled this already buoyant economy and by 1918 New South Wales had the strongest economic base in Australia. This continued until the Great Depression forced the government to protect the economy. The political leader at the time, J. T. Lang, fought running battles with bankers and the Federal government and attempted to repudiate interest payments on state loans which had been generated overseas.

The state Governor, Sir Phillip Game, sacked Lang and in the election that followed the anti-Labor parties won an overwhelming victory. They retained office until the outbreak of World War II when Labor under William McKell regained government. Labor then held power in the state until 1965 when Robert Askin's Liberal-Country Party coalition won a victory which kept them in power for the next nine years. In recent times the Labor Party has held power from 1976 to 1988 when the Liberal-National Coalition under Nick Greiner won government. Labor, under Bob Carr, regained power in 1994 and has been re-elected twice since then.

These relatively long periods of stable government have ensured that progress within the state has been coherent and sustained.

The post-World War II development of the state has seen the construction of the Opera House, the creation of sophisticated urban transport in the Sydney metropolitan area, the development of the vast Snowy Mountains Hydro-Electricity project, the enormous growth of suburban Sydney so that it is now a city similar in size to Los Angeles, and the modernisation of the city centre. The success of New South Wales has been based on the strength and diversity of its economic base and the unchallenged position of Sydney as the financial and industrial capital of Australia.

The diversity of the state's resources ranges from the silver–lead deposits of Broken Hill to the vast coal reserves of the Illawarra and Hunter Valley regions. The cotton growing in the state's north is matched by the huge sheep properties in the west, the rich dairy country along the coast, the cattle and crop country west of the Great Dividing Range and the crops of the Riverina.

Modern changes in technology have resulted in Sydney becoming the home of the major television networks and the headquarters for most national media organisations.

Sydney airport is the primary destination for the majority of overseas flights arriving in Australia and Sydney Harbour, with its Opera House and Harbour Bridge is still regarded as the premier urban tourist attraction in the country.

In 2000 the Olympic Games were held in Sydney after six years of preparation. The games were hailed as an enormous success throughout the world and did a great deal for tourism and Sydney's image throughout the world.

New South Wales is the dominant state in Australia. It is rich and prosperous and with six million residents it accounts for nearly a third of the nation's population.

PREVIOUS PAGE: Bondi Beach in Sydney is Australia's most famous stretch of surf, sand and sunshine. It is one of the thirty-four ocean beaches that the city has to offer.

ABOVE: Two of Sydney's most famous landmarks, the Opera House and the Harbour Bridge, at dusk.

Darling Harbour, covering 54 hectares, is Sydney's most ambitious city development to date. Shown above is the shopping and restaurant complex at night. The bustling recreation and commercial area is a waterfront redevelopment of the former shipping and storage area for the Port of Sydney.

ABOVE: Centrepoint Tower forms a backdrop to the Chinese Gardens on the eastern side of Darling Harbour. The gardens were a gift to the people of Sydney from the people of Guangzhou, Sydney's sister city.

Spanish (above) and scottish dancers (below) perform for the crowds during a daytime multi-cultural performance at Darling Harbour.

ABOVE: The spectacular Sydney Opera House on Bennelong Point was officially opened by Queen Elizabeth II in October 1973—it cost a staggering $102 million to construct.

RIGHT: Rows of colourful and quaint terrace houses at Glebe contrast with modern high rises, creating the juxtaposition that characterises Sydney.

OPPOSITE, ABOVE: Seen from Lavender Bay wharf, the Sydney Harbour Bridge connects the city to the North Shore

OPPOSITE, BELOW: The monorail heads towards Darling Harbour Station from the city.

VISA
10,200 athletes.
1 city. 1 card.

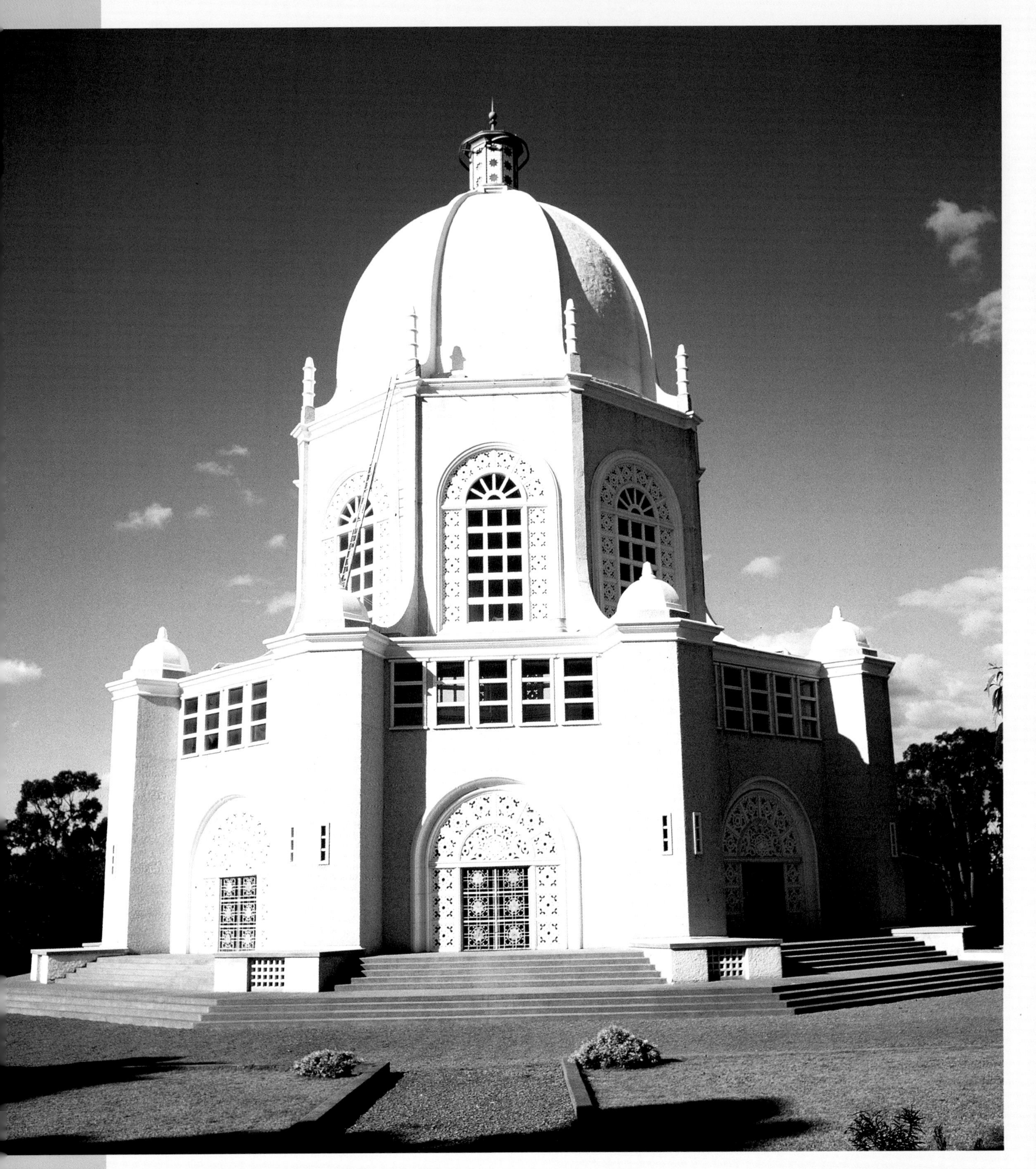

ABOVE: A prominent landmark at Ingleside in Sydney's northern suburbs, the Baha'i House of Worship is a unique nine-sided building rising to a height of 40 metres.

OPPOSITE, TOP: Vaucluse House in Sydney was once home to William Wentworth, one of Australia's most colourful pioneers. Set in beautiful gardens and housing many fine antiques, the mansion is open for public inspection.

OPPOSITE, BOTTOM: Designed by convict architect Francis Greenway in 1821, the Sydney Conservatorium of Music was originally used as horse stables for Government House.

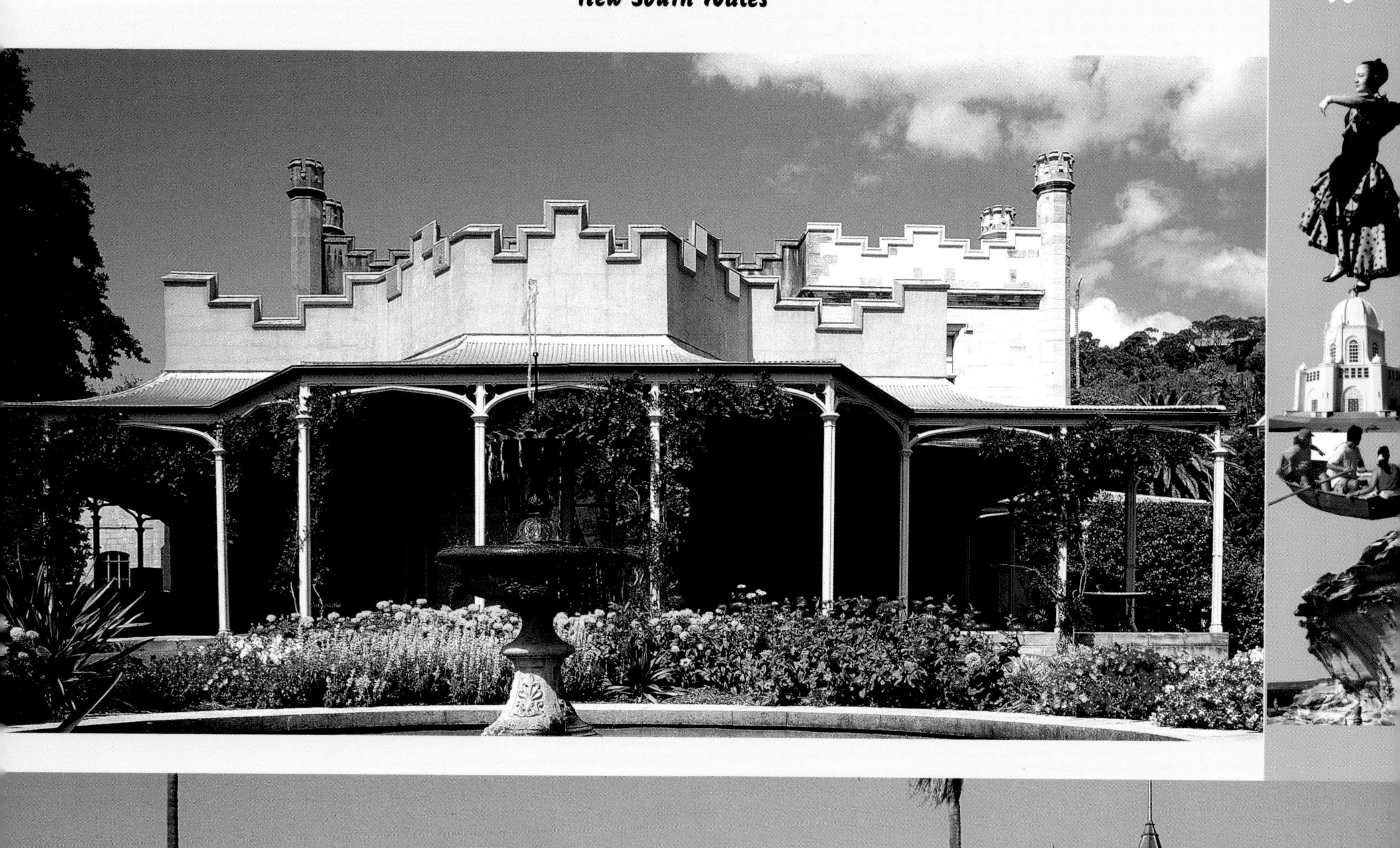

CONSERVATORIUM OF MUSIC
1915

ABOVE: The vast waterways of Sydney's Pittwater and the adjacent Broken Bay are famous for their scenery and gentle boating conditions.

OPPOSITE, TOP: Family boating on the bush-lined Lane Cove River in Sydney.

OPPOSITE, BOTTOM: A huge steel section of the Spit Bridge at Sydney's picturesque Middle Harbour swings up to enable pleasure craft to pass through.

ABOVE: Boating on Lake Macquarie, the largest seaboard lake in Australia.

OPPOSITE: Grand and rugged, with tall stands of timber and natural rock amphitheatres, the Blue Mountains are one of the most impressive scenic attractions within easy reach of Sydney.

BELOW: The General Grocer and Produce store at the historic goldfield site of Hill End.

ABOVE: The Sceniscender at Katoomba in the Blue Mountains, New South Wales, is the steepest cable car in Australia and takes people on a three minute 545 metre ride down into the rainforest.

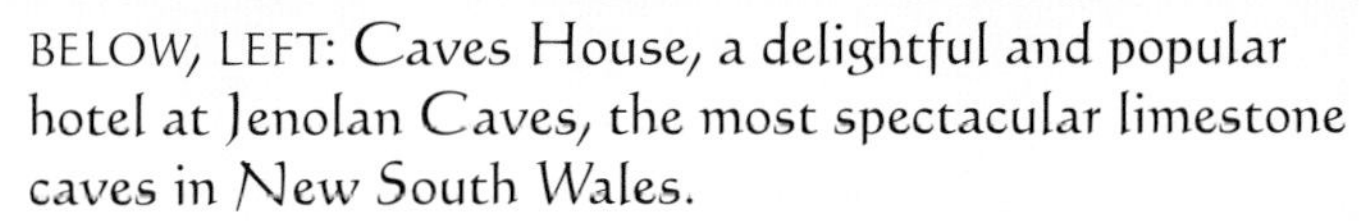

BELOW, LEFT: Caves House, a delightful and popular hotel at Jenolan Caves, the most spectacular limestone caves in New South Wales.

BELOW: Cooma Cottage at Yass, built about 1830, was home to explorer Hamilton Hume who was responsible for opening much of southern New South Wales.

ABOVE: Vibrant gardens at Narrandera, a pastoral and wheat town south-west of Sydney at the gateway of the Murrumbidgee Irrigation area.

BELOW: The old slab huts of New South Wales' early pioneers were honest and simple in design, blending in with the surrounding countryside.

BELOW: Sunset highlights the stark beauty of a natural rock formation near Broken Hill, New South Wales.

ABOVE: Looking over Wollongong from Mt Keira Lookout. This heavily industrialised area is the third largest city in New South Wales.

OPPOSITE: An unusual view of one of the Three Sisters, probably the best known of the sandstone rock formations to be found in the Blue Mountains.

ABOVE: St Matthew's Church, Windsor, is the oldest Anglican church in Australia. Built in 1817, it was designed by convict architect Francis Greenway who was transported to the colony for forgery in 1814.

BELOW: Birds of a feather flock together at The Entrance on the Central Coast of New South Wales.

ABOVE: Rock fishing at the south coast township of Kiama, New South Wales, where the fishing is reputed to be among the best in the country.

BELOW: Magnificent deeply indented coastline and tumbling wooded slopes are features of Bouddi National Park.

ABOVE: The surf rolls in at Flynns Beach, Port Macquarie, one of the oldest towns in the state and now a major holiday resort.

BELOW: Enjoying the ambience of The Entrance, one of the most popular holiday resorts on the Central Coast.

ABOVE: Mt Warning looms behind the picturesque Tweed River near Murwillumbah, in the centre of the banana and sugarcane growing district near the Queensland border.

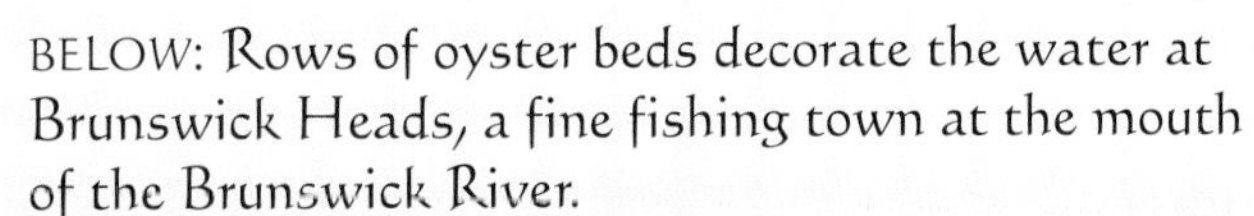

BELOW: Rows of oyster beds decorate the water at Brunswick Heads, a fine fishing town at the mouth of the Brunswick River.

ABOVE: At work at Evans Head fishing port, centre of the New South Wales' prawning industry.

BELOW: Fog shrouds the impressive forest scenery near the timber town of Dorrigo.

BELOW: The convict-built Sea Horse Inn, which still functions as a licensed inn, is one of the few buildings in Boydtown. The town was formerly a rival settlement to Eden and now has little standing, apart from ruins that include a church and lighthouse.

ABOVE: The picturesque fishing town of Ulladulla on the south coast. A colourful ceremony is held here each Easter to bless the fishing fleet.

BELOW: Sunset over the Clyde River at the charming resort town of Batemans Bay on the south coast.

LEFT: Siding Spring Observatory, near the Warrumbungle National Park where the extreme clarity of the air greatly facilitates astronomical observation.

BELOW: Early morning sun highlights the Post Office building in the former goldmining town of Forbes. Bushranger Ben Hall's final resting place is in the town's cemetery.

OPPOSITE: Water lillies enhance the beauty of the Macquarie Marshes.

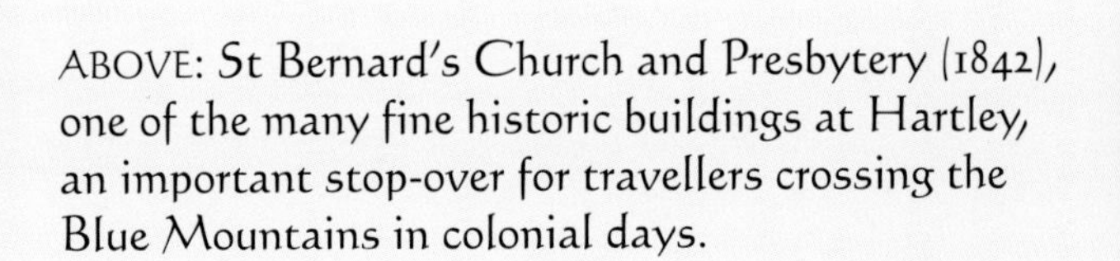

ABOVE: St Bernard's Church and Presbytery (1842), one of the many fine historic buildings at Hartley, an important stop-over for travellers crossing the Blue Mountains in colonial days.

RIGHT: The awesome beauty of Hanging Rock in the Blue Mountains National Park.

ABOVE: Snow sculpted trees at Kosciuszko National Park in the heart of the Snowy Mountains.

LEFT: Early morning fog clothes the town of Tumut on the Snowy Mountains Highway.

RIGHT: The Chalet at Charlotte Pass, a popular ski resort in Kosciuszko National Park. Some of Australia's highest peaks and most spectacular ski runs are accessible from here.

ABOVE: Historic ruins at the ghost town of Silverton where silver chlorides were discovered in 1883.

RIGHT: Opals are mined at the small town of White Cliffs where there is also a walk-in opal mine museum.

OPPOSITE, TOP: Early snowfall at Three Mile Dam in the Snowy Mountains.

OPPOSITE, FAR LEFT: Cattle country at Khancoban near the Snowy Mountains.

OPPOSITE, LEFT: Sunrise throws reflections on one of the huge dams of the Snowy Mountains Hydro-electric Scheme.

OPPOSITE: Spring is bursting out all over this farm track near the pastoral town of Narrandera, south-west of Sydney.

RIGHT: Grape picking in the Hunter Valley, one of Australia's most important wine districts. The country's oldest commercial wine-producing area, wine was first made here in the 1830s.

BELOW: Reminiscent of an English village, historic Carcoar was the scene of New South Wales' first bank hold-up in 1863.

ABOVE: Heavy rainfall plays havoc with road networks in the usually arid wastelands of far western New South Wales.

LEFT: Most magnificent of all Australian wildflowers—the waratah *(Telopea speciosissima)*, floral emblem of the State of New South Wales.

OPPOSITE: Lit by the early morning sun, this ancient rock formation near Tibooburra is a reminder of the extreme age of the Australian continent.

ABOVE: Rolling farmland at Canowindra, a township once commandeered by Ben Hall and his gang of bushrangers.

BELOW: The Civic Theatre at Wagga Wagga, a thriving city on the Murrumbidgee River.

OPPOSITE: Waterfalls cascade through the densely timbered Barrington Tops National Park which straddles the Great Dividing Range.

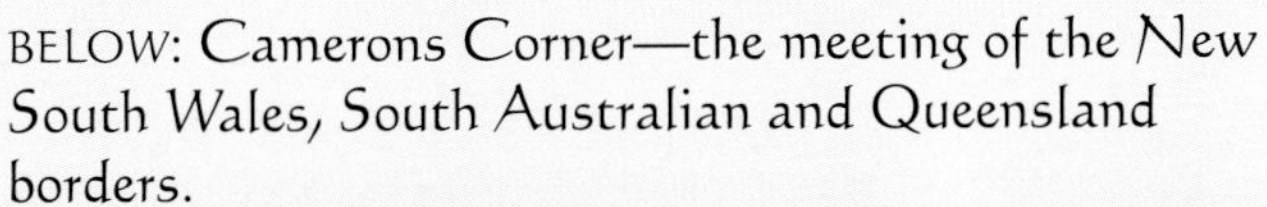

ABOVE: Many of Canowindra's graceful old buildings have been classified by the National Trust.

ABOVE: A great place for a drink—Ettamogah Pub, near Albury.

BELOW: Camerons Corner—the meeting of the New South Wales, South Australian and Queensland borders.

BELOW: The Wall of China—crumbling sedimentary deposits in Mungo National Park in south-western New South Wales.

RIGHT: The War Memorial and a section of the gardens in the Civic Centre at Bathurst in western New South Wales.

BELOW: Nestled between Wollongong and Shell Harbour, Lake Illawarra near Windang is a peaceful retreat.

ABOVE: The beautifully laid out Japanese Gardens and Cultural Centre at Cowra. During World War II Japanese prisoners attempted to escape from a nearby POW camp, 234 of them dying in the struggle. Many committed suicide.

OPPOSITE: The Lachlan Vintage Village at Forbes is a reminder of the past when the bushranger Ben Hall was a frequent visitor to the town.

BELOW: Beautiful gardens in Albury, the principal city of the Murray district.

OPPOSITE: Mellow autumn tones soften a country lane near Tumut, a town with distinctive seasons and ever-changing European treescapes.

BELOW: Berowra Waters, a popular weekend retreat for fishermen and boating enthusiasts, is situated on an arm of the Hawkesbury River.

ABOVE: Golden daffodils form part of colourful spring flower displays in Canberra, A.C.T..

OVERLEAF: A typical Australian skyline—native trees backlit by an impressive sunset.

ABOVE: Duntroon House, the Royal Military College, Canberra, stands on the former Duntroon station, established in 1825 by banker and pastoralist, Robert Campbell.

OPPOSITE: The spectacular Ebor Falls, at Ebor near the New England National Park.

BELOW: Goulburn courthouse is one of the many fine historic buildings in this provincial city, centre of a wealthy farming district.

RIGHT: Sydney's ever-changing harbour scenery, seen here from Elizabeth Bay in the eastern suburbs.

BELOW: The sun sets over Wallis Lake, a popular holiday area of the Great Lakes District, north of Sydney.

ABOVE: Heavily laden golden boughs of the spring flowering Cootamundra wattle (*Acacia baileyana*).

RIGHT: Sunrise over Govetts Leap in the Blue Mountains.

LEFT: Wheat growing is one of the major agricultural activities in New South Wales.

BELOW, LEFT: An old school in the Lachlan Vintage Village, Forbes.

BELOW: The Zig Zag Steam Railway near Lithgow was regarded as an engineering masterpiece when first built in 1868.

BOTTOM: Tebbutt's Observatory, Windsor, was built in 1863 for the distinguished astronomer John Tebbutt who discovered the comet that bears his name.

A breathtaking view over the picturesque Shoalhaven River at Nowra.

OPPOSITE: A mineshaft is silhouetted at Broken Hill in the heart of the rich silver, lead and zinc mining country of the Barrier Range in far western New South Wales.

An early sketch (c. 1912) of Canberra , Australian Capital Territory, as envisaged by its designer, Walter Burley Griffin.

Driving in the first peg at the Commencement Ceremony, 20 February 1913.

The flag of the Australian Capital Territory. Founded as a Federal Territory on 1 January 1911, the Australian Capital Territory attained self-government on 4 March 1989. On 25 March 1993 the pictured flag was adopted by the ACT Legislative Assembly after competitions for a Territory flag had been held during the 1980s and early 1990s. The flag replaced one of a similar design used as the City flag of Canberra and was designed by Ivo Ostyn.

The Australian Capital Territory has adopted the Royal Bluebell as its floral emblem and the Gang Gang Cockatoo (pictured opposite) as its faunal emblem. The Australian Capital Territory has not adopted an animal or marine emblem.

Australian Capital Territory: The Heritage

by Kathrine Bell

Canberra, Australia's National capital is situated on the Monaro tablelands 300 kilometres south-west of Sydney, 653 kilometres north of Melbourne and 130 kilometres from the surfing beaches of the New South Wales south coast. Designed on a grand scale as the seat of government of the Commonwealth of Australia it is also a centre for learning and the arts. It is a city of rare beauty with sweeping tree-lined avenues, grand buildings and monuments set in wide areas of landscaped parkland along the shores of an ornamental waterway, Lake Burley Griffin.

Canberra's story began before Federation when the architects of the constitution dreamed of a city which would be the focal point and the tangible symbol representing the union of the six states.

The latter half of the nineteenth century was a period of great social and economic change throughout Australia. The individual colonies, by achieving responsible government, had increased in stature and the scars caused by the evils of the penal system had begun to fade. Gold had been discovered in New South Wales and Victoria during the 1850s which resulted in a rapid increase in population. Settlement of the interior of the continent had followed on the heels of the explorers, and the cities, enriched by the wealth from the goldfields, prospered and grew.

The colonial yoke was becoming heavy and a new spirit of nationalism was emerging. The concept of a federal union had been strongly advocated for some years by Sir Henry Parkes, the Premier of New South Wales, who maintained that 'the crimson thread' of kinship would ultimately bind the colonies together under the title of his choosing, the Commonwealth of Australia. Although at first the idea appeared to be impractical, it gained support and the last decade of the nineteenth century was a decade of steady progress towards this end.

During the drafting of the constitution in the 1890s, the vexed question of the selection and situation of the capital arose. This caused differences of opinion amongst the colonial governments. The existing cities of Sydney and Melbourne, by virtue of age and population, both considered their right to be chosen as absolute and this resulted in a spate of arguments between New South Wales and Victoria.

The disagreement resulted in a threat by New South Wales to abandon the proposed Commonwealth. A convention held in Melbourne in 1899 attempted to settle the question inserting a provision in the Constitution which stated clearly that the capital was to be in New South Wales on a site chosen by Parliament and situated not less

The Naming of Canberra Ceremony, 12 March 1913.

from London that from 1 January 1901, one hundred and thirteen years after Governor Phillip and his miserable band of convicts had landed at Sydney Cove, the six colonies would become the Commonwealth of Australia, a nation under one flag but within the ambit of the British Empire.

It was anticipated that Federation would be the beginning of a new era of achievement and progress and so the inaugural ceremonies were conducted in an atmosphere of excited euphoria. Pageants and parades were organised, flags and bunting adorned the city streets, and the nation celebrated with patriotic fervour. On 9 May 1901 the first Federal Parliament was opened by their Royal Highnesses the Duke (later King George V) and Duchess of Cornwall and York at the Melbourne Exhibition Building. It was a grand occasion attended by a large assembly of dignitaries, but it served to emphasise to Prime Minister Edmond Barton and his ministers the lack of a permanent home for Federal Parliament.

The selection of a site for the national capital was an urgent matter which needed to be resolved as quickly as possible. However, progress was slow. Many areas in New South Wales were examined and for one reason or another were found to be unsuitable. An argument developed between New South Wales and the Commonwealth over the transfer of the as yet unselected site and differences arose among the various ministers as to the merits or otherwise of each site under discussion.

In 1908 the selection was narrowed down to two areas, Dalgety and Yass-Canberra. In the final count Yass-Canberra won by eight votes. In 1909

than 160 kilometres from Sydney in territory which was to be ceded to the Commonwealth Government by the State. To mollify Victoria, Melbourne was chosen as the seat of government until Parliament House was established in the new capital. Peace was restored.

On 9 July 1900 the Commonwealth of Australia Constitution Act received the Royal Assent from H. M. Queen Victoria after passing through the British House of Commons for ratification. Western Australia was not included at this time as a problem had arisen there regarding the abolition of Customs duty between the states. This fact was a matter of some concern as the collection of excise duty was a valuable source of revenue and its loss could have a detrimental effect on the economy of Western Australia.

However, a referendum was held in July 1900 which tipped the scales in favour of union with the eastern states and with this the last milestone on the road to Federation was passed and the final step into nationhood was about to be taken. On 17 September 1900 it was officially announced the Seat of Government Act confirming the selection of the Yass-Canberra site was passed by Parliament and in that year a survey to determine the boundaries of the proposed Federal territory was requested by the Commonwealth Government. This was undertaken by a New South Wales government surveyor Charles Robert Scrivener who was also asked to recommend a site within the territory for the new capital. He was given specific guidelines on which to base his selection:

> The surveyor will bear in mind that the federal capital should be a beautiful city occupying a commanding position with extensive views, and embracing distinctive features, which will lend themselves to the evolution of a design worthy of the object, not only for the present, but for all time; consequently the potentialities of the site will demand most careful consideration from an hygienic standpoint, with a view to securing picturesqueness, and also with the object of beautification and expansion.

HRH the Prince of Wales dedicating the foundation stone of the present Parliament House on Capitol Hill in June 1920. The building was finally completed and opened in 1988

The site selected by Scrivener had been known from the pioneer days as the Limestone Monaro or Canberry Plains. It was a narrow stretch of fertile grazing land intersected by the meanderings of the Molonglo River, encircled by gently rolling wooded hills and fringed in the distance by the cloud-capped escarpments and wild gullies of the Brindabella Range. Nestled snugly on the floor of the valley stood the historic Church of St John the Baptist which in 1909 was over 60 years old.

Settlement of the district had followed swiftly in the wake of the explorers Joseph Wild, James Vaughan and Charles Throsby Smith who in 1820 had crossed the Canberra site in an unsuccessful search for the Murrumbidgee River. The river was discovered the following year by Smith's uncle Dr Charles Throsby, an ex-naval surgeon who owned a property near Liverpool. He was interested in exploration and had become deeply involved with the opening up of land for settlement in the south and south-west districts of New South Wales. He was followed in 1823 by Captain Mark Currie R.N., and Brigade Major John Ovens (who discovered Isabella Plains, later to be named Tuggeranong), and in 1824 by the Botanist Allan Cunningham.

The glowing reports brought back by the explorers of rich grazing land soon attracted attention and by the end of 1824 the employees of John Joshua Moore were building stockyards on Canberry Station between Black Mountain and the Molonglo River. Moore was followed in 1825 by Robert Campbell whose manager James Ainslie established Duntroon which was to become one of the largest properties in the district.

As the nineteenth century progressed more settlers arrived to take up land; the Macphersons and Sullivans of Springbank, the Murrays and the Gibbes of Yarralumla, the De Salis family of Cuppacumbalong, the Wrights and the Cunning-

The opening of the Federal Parliament in Canberra on 11 May 1927. These temporary buildings were replaced by the permanent House of Parliament buildings opened in 1988.

hams of Lanyon, the Kayes of Klesendorlffe Farm, the Webbs of Tidbinbilla and Uriarra, the Southwells of Parkwood Ginninderra, the Shumacks of Springvale Weetangera, William Davis of Ginninderra and Gungahlin plus others whose names have long been associated with the pioneer days.

In those early times there was no indication that the spotlight of history with its clear bright light would focus on this valley. However, in 1909 the Commonwealth Government and the New South Wales Government simultaneously passed respectively, the Seat of Government Acceptance Act and the Seat of Government Surrender Act. Thus the district was swept into the centre of the stage.

On 1 January 1911 the Commonwealth Government took formal possession of the area now known as the Australian Capital Territory plus a small portion of land at Jervis Bay on the south coast of New South Wales which was to serve as an outlet to the sea.

During 1911 an international competition was launched to find a suitable design for the construction of the new national capital. This was won in 1912 by Walter Burley Griffin an architect from Chicago who had worked in close association with Frank Lloyd Wright whose controversial designs were well known in the United States. Griffin's plan was an unusual one and bore no resemblance to the accepted pattern which in those days still leaned towards the ordered flamboyance of the Victorian era. It consisted of a series of circular avenues radiating from a central point with the dominant feature being a large triangular section reserved for the construction of buildings of national importance. These buildings would be spaced along the shores of an artificial waterway to be created in the heart of the city.

On 12 March 1913 the Commonwealth ceremony was held at the site and Lady Denman, wife of the Governor-General, officially named the Capital, Canberra, ending the speculation about a name which had been rife throughout the nation during the preceding year. It was a popular although not altogether a unanimous choice, as many names had been considered. Some were ridiculous such as Sydmeladeperbrisho, some were humorous and others, such as Perfection were abstract. Emu, Possum and Kookaburra though suggested were not considered suitable. Myola was favoured by the Prime Minister. The name Canberra is thought to be derived from an Aboriginal word meaning 'meeting place' and is particularly appropriate as the district had been known as Canberry or Canberra from the earliest European pioneer days.

Although Griffin was awarded the prize-money

by King O'Malley, the Minister for Home Affairs, some government officials were of the opinion that the design was impractical and would be too costly to construct, so an alternative plan was drawn up by a departmental board.

In view of this Burley Griffin was not present at the Commencement ceremony. However, a new government was elected late that year under the Labor leader Andrew Fisher and Burley Griffin was invited to Canberra to take up the position of Federal Director of Design and Construction, and the alternative plan was dropped. This was not a popular decision among some government officials and Griffin was constantly harassed by difficulties and delays. To make things worse World War I had broken out and there was little money to spare for the construction of the city. Nevertheless some progress was made and Griffin spent time revising his original plan and laying the groundwork of the design. The final revised design was gazetted in 1918 and forms the basis of the Canberra of today.

In 1921 Griffin was invited to join the Federal Capital Advisory Board which had been formed to expedite the city's development but he declined and severed his connection with Canberra.

In the interval between World War I and II a concerted effort was made to progress construction to the point where some government departments could function in the capital. This was partly successful. The Parliamentary staff was transferred to prepare for the opening of the new Parliament House in 1927 but shortly after this the first tremors which heralded the onset of the Great Depression of the 1930s were felt. This again impeded further progress, although plans were in hand for the building of the Australian War Memorial which was commenced in 1934. The outbreak of World War II forced further cutbacks but by this time most government departments were permanently in residence in the capital. In 1945 the population was only 13 000 still far short of the total of 25 000 on which Burley Griffin's plan was based. It was during this postwar period that Canberra's growth-rate accelerated to an enormous degree. By 1958 the population had reached 39 000 and was still rising and in that year the National Capital Development Commission was formed on the recommen-

When this photograph was taken in 1955 Canberra was still sparsely populated. Lake Burley Griffin and the great buildings on its southern shore were yet to be completed as were the Department of Defence buildings at Russell. A huge expansion was to follow from the 1960s to the present day.

The Ceremony to celebrate the opening of the Royal Australian Mint at Deakin in February 1965.

dation of a Senate Committee, for the purpose of controlling and planning all aspects of the city's future development.

The projects undertaken by the Commission have been monumental and include most of the buildings in the national area, housing estates, educational facilities, community and shopping centres, restoration of historic buildings and a general beautification of the city as a whole. One of the most important of its functions has been the planning and construction of satellite townships in the surrounding district which have been created as a decentralisation measure.

Canberra has never been constructed as a centre for heavy industrial growth but nevertheless provision was made for the establishment of some light industry. Fishwyck, the first of these light industrial centres, was created in 1954. Mitchell, which is close to Gungahlin near the Federal and Barton Highways, Belconnen West and Jerrabomberra followed during the 1970s and 1980s.

In the twenty-first century, Canberra is truly the National Capital. With the completion and official opening of Parliament House on Capitol Hill in 1988, the great vision of Walter Burley Griffin became finally apparent. The last piece was in place and now the city has truly been able to take its place as one of the great world architectural and planning masterpieces of its time. No news broadcast or telecast is complete without information from the Federal Capital which usually takes first place in news bulletins around the country. Visitors can enjoy the concentric circular streets planted with more than four million native and exotic trees and shrubs. Cosmopolitan restaurants and the international flavour of diplomatic missions have introduced an interesting ambience to the city. Add to this the impressive public buildings and absorbing museums and galleries and it can be readily seen why Canberra attracts increasingly large numbers of visitors from all around the country, and indeed from the whole world.

ABOVE: The Australian flag flies proudly atop the modern Parliament House on Capitol Hill in Canberra.

RIGHT: Shoppers relax under autumn foliage in Petrie Place near the huge Monaro Mall shopping complex in Canberra.

LEFT: Tranquil Lake Burley Griffin, around which the model city of Canberra has been developed, was created by the damming of a tributory of the Murrumbidgee River. In the background, the Telecommunications Tower rises 195.2 metres above ground level on the summit of Black Mountain.

ABOVE: The fifty-three bells of the Canberra Carillon regularly resound over the shores of Lake Burley Griffin. The Carillon was given to Australia by the British Government to mark the Jubileee of the founding of Canberra and stands on Aspen Island in Lake Burley Griffin. It provides regular Sunday afternoon recitals.

OPPOSITE, TOP: Blundell's Farmhouse in Canberra was built in 1858 by the Campbells of Duntroon for a ploughman employed on the property. It was later occupied by the Blundells who worked the small surrounding farm for fifty years.

OPPOSITE, LEFT: The dome-shaped Academy of Science building in Canberra is surrounded by a water-filled moat.

OPPOSITE, FAR LEFT: The foundation stone of the historic Anglican Church of St John the Baptist in Canberra was laid in 1841. The church is built entirely from local materials and contains many memorials to those of Canberra's pioneer past.

ABOVE: A drawcard for young and old, the fascinating model English village of Cockington Green is one of Canberra's most famous attractions.

Brighton Beach in the 1880s.

The Pier and Esplanade, St Kilda c. 1886.

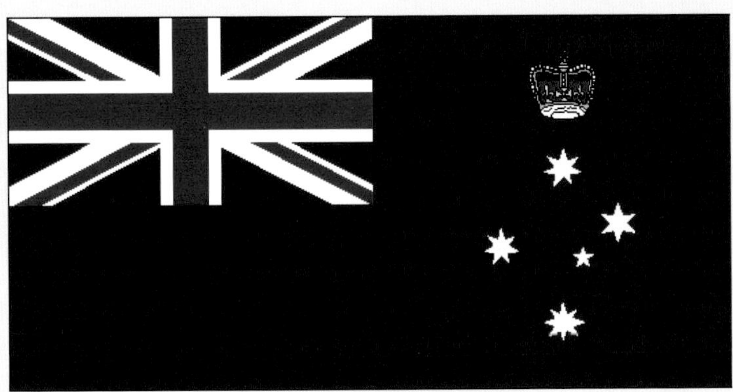

The flag of Victoria (the Garden State).
This flag was adopted c. 1953 and is basically a British Blue Ensign with the state badge sitting on a blue background. The badge displays the Southern Cross surmounted by the St Edward's Crown. The stars in the Southern Cross range from six to eight points. The design of the flag is changed in accordance with the style of Crown chosen by the reigning monarch. The last change occured in 1953 after Queen Elizabeth II adopted the St Edward's Crown at her Coronation in 1952.

Victoria has adopted the common heath (pictured opposite) as its floral emblem, the helmeted honeyeater as its faunal emblem and Leadbeater's possum as its animal emblem. Victoria has not yet adopted a marine emblem.

Victoria: The Heritage

by Bruce Elder

Victoria enjoys a unique position in Australian history. Until 1851 it was part of New South Wales. Then, in a period of forty years, it rapidly became the premier state due to the vast wealth which was being generated by its goldfields. This wealth turned Melbourne into the financial and administrative centre of Australia, a position which the city enjoyed at the time of federation and which it managed to retain until the 1960s and 1970s. Up until this time the head offices of many federal government departments and most of the country's largest companies were still based in the city.

Like most Australian colonies the original reason for the British occupation of Victoria was the fear of possible French settlement. By the end of the eighteenth century the coast had been explored extensively by both British and French adventurers. Reacting to a perceived French threat Lieutenant David Collins, accompanied by a party comprising both convicts and free settlers, landed on the shores of Port Phillip (near the modern-day site of Sorrento) in October 1803 and a short-lived colony was established. By May 1804 Collins had gained permission to move the colony to Van Diemen's Land and his brief attempt at settlement had been abandoned.

Through the 1810s and 1820s Port Phillip was regularly visited by whalers and sealers who worked the coast from Van Diemen's Land to South Australia.

The real impetus for permanent settlement came as a result of the land-based explorers who, having explored south from Sydney, had crossed the Murrumbidgee River and pushed on towards the southern coast. Hume and Hovell reached Port Phillip in 1824. They mistook it for Western Port and two years later, acting on their incorrect advice, a military and convict outpost was established on Western Port. It lasted thirteen months.

Around this time the entrepreneurial John Batman, who was living in Van Diemen's Land, tried to gain approval from the Governor of New South Wales to settle the area around Western Port. He had been encouraged by reports that the land was fertile and the pastures rich. The Governor, fearing problems if a second colony was created, denied Batman permission. This proved to be a hollow gesture. Eight years later, in November 1834, Edward Henty ignored the rulings of the New South Wales Governor and settled at Portland Bay. In early 1835, spurred on by Henty's example, Batman crossed Bass Strait and in June 1835 infamously 'purchased' the land on the western shore of Port Phillip from the local Aborigines.

At this time Batman explored the shores of Port Phillip and chose a site for a village. Within a year

Boating on the Yarra in the 1880s.

the township of Melbourne began to grow on the banks of the Yarra River.

The subsequent exploration of Victoria occurred quite rapidly. The New South Wales Surveyor-General, Major T. L. Mitchell, traversed Victoria in 1836 establishing routes to the Upper Murray and pushing through to Portland Bay. The settlement which followed was rapid. By 1845 squatters, following the lead of Edward Henty, had occupied nearly all of the Western District, settled along the Murray River and, led by Angus McMillan, moved down into the Gippsland area. Effectively the state, although it was still part of New South Wales, had been settled in 1850.

In 1837 the township of Melbourne was surveyed and named and a magistrate, Captain William Lonsdale, was sent from Sydney to maintain law and order. The attempts to stop settlement had clearly failed and the administration of New South Wales was forced to deal with Victoria as a successful, and semi-autonomous, colony. This was converted into a reality in September 1839 when Charles La Trobe, the newly appointed Superintendant of the Port Phillip District, arrived from England. In his wake the colony established a separate police force, a customs office and, perhaps most importantly, a separate Lands Office.

By 1 July 1851, when the colony of Victoria was officially proclaimed, there were already more than 80 000 people living south of the Murray–Murrumbidgee and over six million sheep were being grazed on well-established properties.

In theory, Victoria would have remained a rural economy (although in 1851 it was true that more than 20 000 of the state's 80 000 people were living in Melbourne) but the discovery of gold changed everything.

The gold discoveries in New South Wales had attracted labourers north to the goldfields around Bathurst. This trend was short lived. By November 1851 alluvial gold had been discovered at Clunes, Anderson's Creek, Buninyong, Ballarat, Mount Alexander and Bendigo, which at the time was known as Sandhurst. Gold fever had struck the state. The streets of Melbourne were virtually deserted and, by early 1852, ships from all over the world were disgorging eager miners on the wharves of Melbourne.

By 1854 the colony's population had grown from 80 000 to 300 000, the value of imported goods had reached an extraordinary £18 million, and everything needed for mining, from food to houses and equipment, was being shipped into the colony. In 1856 more than 86 million grams of gold were mined. This would form the basis for unprecedented development which would establish

Melbourne as Australia's major financial centre and Victoria as an extremely wealthy colony.

A total of more than £100 million worth of gold was won from the earth in the 1850s. As it happened, this was not without its problems. The early supplies of alluvial gold disappeared and companies were quickly formed to extract the ore. The government, eager to cash in on the goldfields, established an expensive licence fee which had to be paid by every miner regardless of their success. The licence fee became a major source of discontent with local administrations seeming to use it to harass miners. The situation boiled over into the closest thing Australia has ever had to civil war. On 3 December 1854 a group of miners, led by Peter Lalor, fought a brief and bloody battle with government forces at the Eureka Stockade on the Ballarat goldfields. Thirty men were killed and a large number of agitators were subsequently arrested. When they were brought before the courts in Melbourne the juries refused to convict them. This was symbolic of the complex and radical forces which were working in the colony at the time.

Victoria's development was dramatically different from other colonies in the sense that its independence coincided with huge wealth, huge influxes of migrants and rapid changes in the nature of the society.

In 1855 a Legislative Council and Legislative Assembly were created to administer the colony. The problem was that membership and voting rights were tied to ownership of substantial tracts of land. Thus, the first parliament was made up almost entirely of lawyers, successful businessmen, affluent squatters and merchants. They may have represented the 80 000 people who lived in the state in 1851 but they hardly represented the 300 000 in 1855.

The Legislative Assembly politicians were sufficiently aware of the changing face of Victorian society that, with admirable pragmatism, they introduced a series of reforms. In 1856 Victoria saw the introduction of the secret ballot (possibly the first in the world), the following year universal male suffrage was introduced and in 1870 the parliament agreed that parliamentary members should be paid.

The Exhibition buildings in the 1880s.

Unfortunately the members of the colony's Legislative Council were less flexible. In spite of the changes in the lower house this upper house remained a bastion of conservatism and exclusivity with membership restricted to males with more than £5000 in property. They were elected to ten-year terms. They remained an anachronism unable to meet the changing circumstances of the colony.

Similar tensions began to emerge on the goldfields as different cultures confronted each other. The Chinese were the brunt of racist attacks. By 1855 there were 17 000 Chinese in Victoria and most of them were working on the goldfields. The diggers, looking for someone to blame as the easy wealth of the fields dried up, turned their anger on the Chinese. The Victorian parliament introduced a series of particularly offensive pieces of racist legislation which would eventually form the basis for the White Australia Policy.

As the diggings declined the government had to deal with the problem of unemployed miners. The government offered a range of incentives to try to encourage miners to turn to farming. While it was fraught with problems the arrangement was basically successful. By the 1890s large areas of

The Drive, Albert Park as it would have appeared in about 1886.

The vitality and dynamism of the state continued after World War II with rapid rural growth being accompanied by successful and sustained industrial and manufacturing success. By 1992 the state's population was 4 458 895. Victoria had attracted large numbers of non-English-speaking settlers (particularly from Italy and Greece) and they had impacted significantly on the character of the state. Lygon Street in Melbourne, famed for its international cuisine, is a symbol of the cultural diversity of the city.

Victoria had been cleared and wool and wheat dominated the rural economy.

Inevitably, the wealth generated by gold could not be sustained. The state experienced a major economic downturn in the last two decades of the nineteenth century. It recovered in the early years of the twentieth century when the combination of successful exporting of dairy products, expanding open-cut coal mining in Gippsland, and significant growth in the state's manufacturing sector ensured economic stability.

This economic recovery established a stable base. After World War I, when imports were in short supply, the Victorian economy expanded rapidly to meet local demands. Unfortunately, the success of the manufacturing sector had an unforeseen effect. The Great Depression decimated the sector and by October 1931 more than 25 per cent of the state's workforce were unemployed and over 170 000 people were dependent on welfare assistance. The situation was not helped by the success of the newly emergent Country Party which was committed to the problems of rural workers and less interested in the problems the Depression had created for urban workers.

It seemed as though the tensions which had emerged after the goldrushes—the tensions between radicalism and conservatism, the tensions between established rural landowners and 'get-rich-quick' entrepreneurs, the tensions between primary producers and manufacturers—were to be enduring characteristics of Victoria's personality and character.

In the late 1980s Victoria experienced severe economic problems. A recession, combined with a series of spectacular corporate and financial institution collapses, ensured that the state's Labor government which had come to power in 1982 after twenty-seven years of Liberal rule, was swept from office.

The new Liberal government under Jeff Kennett, instituted a strict economic regime to rein in state expenditure. After initial resistance the state accepted the 'harsh medicine' with the result that, while still experiencing considerable economic problems, the state enjoyed a welcome return to confidence and stability. Kennett had fulfilled his promise of restoring the state to a healthy financial condition. Unfortunately for Kennett though, he forgot or ignored his supporters in the country regions and the inevitable result was that despite his reforms, he lost government. The present government of Steve Bracks started as a minority Labor government with the support of independents in its first term but now in its second, governs successfully in its own right.

These days, Melbourne, with its modern buildings and rejuvenated river bank precincts, enjoys a reputation for great food, sophisticated leisure and arts appreciation and is high on the world list of city tourist destinations.

ABOVE: Enjoy international food, a scenic tour and the ambience of a historic wooden tram on Melbourne's Colonial Tramcar Restaurant.

BELOW: Melbourne's Exhibition Building—originally built for the Great Exhibition in 1880, this grandiose domed hall is still used for trade fairs.

ABOVE: The two massive black Rialto towers loom over the historic Rialto Hotel, reflecting Melbourne's old wealth and modern-day prosperity.

BELOW: The pyramid-style Shrine of Remembrance dominates Kings Domain, Melbourne.

OVERLEAF: The Great Ocean Road snakes for 300 kilometres along the scenic south-west coast of Victoria. Carved into the cliffside to honour the servicemen of World War I, it is one of the world's greatest coastal roads.

ABOVE: Melbourne, capital of Victoria, overlooks the Yarra River. Founded by John Batman in 1835, it is today an elegant cosmopolitan city.

OPPOSITE: Westgate Bridge spans the Yarra River, Melbourne.

ABOVE: On the hop—kangaroos in western Victoria.

BELOW: The wharf at the river city of Echuca, once Australia's largest inland port.

BELOW: Sovereign Hill, a reconstruction of a goldmining settlement, is a major tourist attraction just outside the centre of Ballarat.

ABOVE: The Chinese Joss House, Bendigo, was built by the many Chinese miners who worked the gold diggings here.

BELOW: Paddlesteamers depart from Mildura wharf on trips up and down the Murray and Darling rivers.

ABOVE: Sailing at Brighton on Port Phillip Bay.

BELOW: Open to the public—'Hymettus', a prize-winning cottage garden in Ballarat.

Skiers on the slopes of Mt Buller in the Victorian Alps.

LEFT: The Organ Pipes—a series of hexagonal basalt columns that rise more than 20 metres above Jacksons Creek at Organ Pipes National Park. They were formed when lava cooled in an ancient river bed.

OPPOSITE: Autumn colours in the 40-hectare Botanic Gardens at Ballarat.

BELOW: Fishing boats at the popular holiday town of Lakes Entrance at the eastern end of the Gippsland Lakes. Victoria's commercial fishing industry is dominated by scallop and abalone.

OVERLEAF: London Bridge, an unusual rock structure sculpted out of soft limestone cliffs by the pounding sea at Port Campbell.

LEFT: Famous bushranger Ned Kelly's last stand at Glenrowan. Ned was captured here after a bloody gunfight and was subsequently condemned and hanged in Melbourne.

BELOW: Erskine Falls in the scenic Otway Ranges behind the coastal resort of Lorne.

RIGHT: Wildflowers bloom near the Cathedral in Mt Buffalo National Park. More than 400 species of plants and flowers are found on this high granite plateau.

BELOW: Trout fishing in the Ovens River.

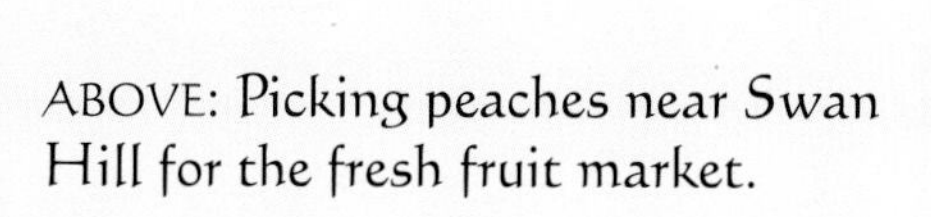

ABOVE: Picking peaches near Swan Hill for the fresh fruit market.

OPPOSITE: Victoria's most imposing national park, the Grampians, is a series of high weathered ridges forming the westernmost heights of the Great Dividing Range.

RIGHT: Petrified forest at Cape Bridgewater near Portland.

ABOVE: Crayfish catch at the holiday resort town Port Fairy, home to a large fishing fleet and once one of the biggest ports in Australia.

BELOW: Chateau Tahbilk, built in 1860, is one of the most picturesque wineries in the Goulburn River Valley.

ABOVE: Ready for shearing at a property in the Western District, an area which supports one-third of Victoria's best sheep and cattle.

OPPOSITE: Mount William, the highest peak in the Grampians, was climbed by Major Mitchell in 1836. He named the ranges after the Grampians in his native Scotland.

BELOW: An oldtimer relaxes at the Swan Hill Pioneer Settlement, a reconstruction of the days when paddle-steamers were the Murray Valley's main form of transport.

ABOVE: Puffing Billy is Australia's oldest surviving steam railway. It was the last of the experimental narrow-gauge railway lines built at the turn of the 20th century to help develop rural areas. It carries passengers on a 25-kilometre journey through forests and gullies from Belgrave to Emerald Lake Park and Gembrook.

BELOW : Healesville Sanctuary in the Yarra Valley features more than 200 species of native birds, mammals and reptiles in walk-through habitats and enclosures.

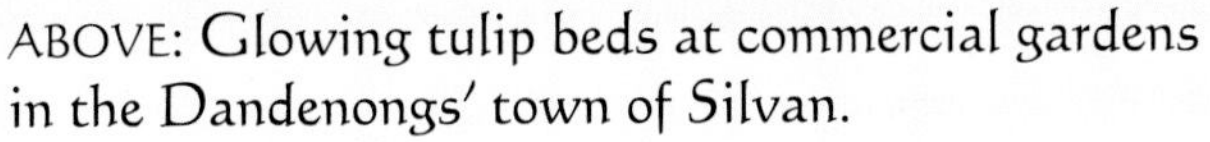

ABOVE: Glowing tulip beds at commercial gardens in the Dandenongs' town of Silvan.

OPPOSITE: Surf fishing on the beautiful Ninety Mile Beach which separates the lakes from the ocean in the Gippsland region.

ABOVE: Sunset at Squeaky Beach on Wilsons Promontory.

OPPOSITE: The spectacularly eroded coastline of Port Campbell, scene of many shipwrecks in the late nineteenth century.

BELOW: A tidal river at Wilsons Promontary National Park.

LEFT: South East Point, on the tip of the rugged, densely vegetated Wilsons Promontory.

OPPOSITE: Sweeping views over the Grampians range from the 'Jaws of Death'.

BELOW: The many English and European trees bring spectacular autumn colours to the town of Bright in the heart of the beautiful Ovens Valley.

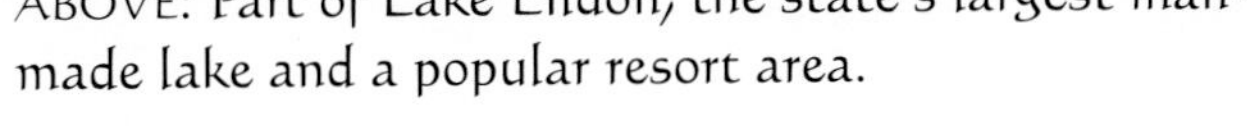

ABOVE: Part of Lake Eildon, the state's largest man-made lake and a popular resort area.

ABOVE: Waterfalls, ferny rainforest and walking tracks are features of Tarra Valley National Park near Morwell.

BELOW: Fog softens the scene at Lake Wendouree near Ballarat.

BELOW: Harvesting grain in the Wimmera region, the granary of the state, where wheatfields stretch as far as the eye can see.

ABOVE: Rocky reflections at Whisky Beach, Wilsons Promontory, at the southernmost tip of the Australian mainland.

RIGHT: Temperate rainforest in the charming Lilly Pilly Gully in Wilsons Promontory National Park.

ABOVE: At work on a fishing net at Portland, the only deep-water port between Melbourne and Adelaide.

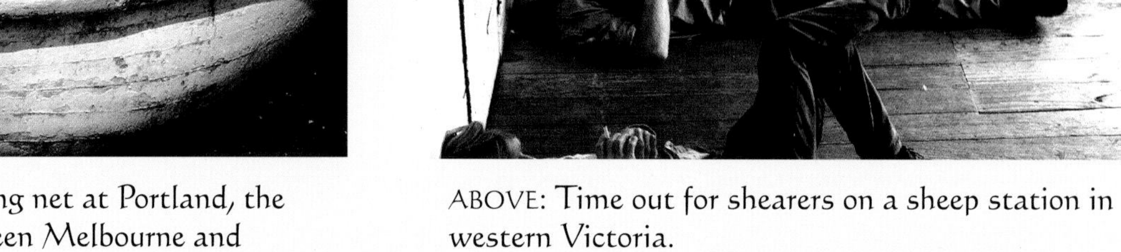

ABOVE: Time out for shearers on a sheep station in western Victoria.

BELOW: Gathering seed on a flower farm at Leopold.

ABOVE: Thompson's seedless grapes—grown for export and fresh fruit markets. Victoria's main grape-growing area is centred around Rutherglen and extends down into the Ovens and Goulburn Valleys.

BELOW: Dramatic coastal scenery near Peterborough.

ABOVE: The annual vintage farm display at Nhill, a small wheat town halfway between Melbourne and Adelaide.

OVERLEAF: Bird's eye view of the fishing township of Mallacoota on the Gippsland coast.

ABOVE: Charming old buildings are testament to the prosperity of the gold boom era in Ballarat.

OPPOSITE: Futuristic architecture of the Daimaru complex in Melbourne.

Below: A riot of colour in the Warrnambool Gardens.

ABOVE: Bottle-lined cellars in a winery at the small town of Great Western which has given its name to many fine wines.

OVERLEAF: The Horn, a feature of the Mount Buffalo National Park, north-east of Melbourne. Granite tors, rounded boulders and massive rock formations make up the landscape of this park.

ABOVE: Triathlon at the flourishing coastal resort of Warrnambool.

OPPOSITE: Triplet Falls, tumbling in three stages through rainforest bushland, are one of the many waterfalls found in the steep slopes and tall forests of the Otway Ranges which merge with the Southern ocean to form a 12 876 hectare national park in Victoria.

Hobart in the 1880s.

The Fountain, Launceston c. 1886.

The flag of Tasmania (the Holiday Isle).
This flag was approved in 1875 by the British Colonial office. Except for a slight alteration in the rendition of the lion in 1975 when the flag was officially proclaimed the 'Tasmanian Flag', the design has not changed since its approval.
The flag consists of a British Blue Ensign with the state badge sitting on a blue background. The badge displays a red lion passant on a white disc but the exact symbolism of this is unknown.

Tasmania has unofficially adopted the well-known tasmanian devil (pictured opposite) as its animal emblem and the tasmanian blue gum as its floral emblem. Tasmania has not yet adopted a marine or faunal emblem.

Tasmania: The Heritage

by Bruce Elder

Tasmania's history is one of hardship and struggle on a tiny isolated island at the end of the world. It is so totally different from the rest of Australia that there have been times when mainlanders have ignored its existence.

Tasmania is wet and cold where the mainland is predominantly hot and dry. It is intimate and undulating; the mainland is flat and expansive. It is European in its style; the mainland is aggressively Australian and post-colonial.

Over and over again Tasmania's history has run counter to the events which were unfolding on the mainland. When Sydney Town was thriving, the settlement at Hobart Town was struggling. When pastoralists were opening up the vast grazing lands of eastern Australia, Tasmanians were struggling with small acreages between Hobart and George Town.

When eastern Australia was gripped by gold fever, Tasmania was dealing with both a depression and a political crisis. In the 1980s when the world was rapidly embracing environmental concerns, Tasmania was still committed to drowning wilderness areas for hydro-electric dams and felling forests for wood chip and paper manufacture. In the twenty-first century, Tasmania appears to be gradually going through a metamorphosis. Entrenched attitudes to the gay and lesbian movement have altered and more Tasmanians are becoming committed to modern environmental practices. Retired mainlanders are beginning to see Tasmania as an attractive alternative to urban city dwelling and with the baby-boomer generation edging towards retirement, it is likely that the process of change will continue.

There is no easy answer to why Tasmania was so different from the rest of Australia for so long. The combination of Bass Strait (which is a formidable barrier), a history of hardship, a small population and a fragile economic base has resulted in a deep conservatism produced by a perception that Tasmania is permanently in danger of economic collapse.

It is believed that Aborigines first arrived in Tasmania about 30–40 000 years ago. Between 10 000 and 6500 years ago the sea level between Tasmania and the mainland rose. This meant that the people trapped on the island were isolated from all contact until the arrival of European explorers in the seventeenth and eighteenth centuries.

The first European to reach Tasmania was the Dutch navigator and explorer, Abel Tasman. Sailing from Batavia he landed on the east coast

Cataract Hill, Launceston in the 1880s.

of Tasmania in 1642 and, not knowing he was on an island, took possession of the land naming it in honour of Anthony Van Diemen, the Governor-General of the Dutch East Indies.

No further exploration of the island took place for the next 130 years. Then, at the end of the eighteenth century, in quick succession, the island was visited by Marion du Fresne (1772) Furneaux (1773), Cook (1777), Bligh (1788), J. H. Cox (1789), Bruni d'Entrecasteaux and Huon de Kermadec (1792–93) and John Hayes (1793). It wasn't until 1798–99 that Bass and Flinders circumnavigated the island.

The too-frequent visits by French explorers concerned the British authorities in both Sydney and London. In 1803 it was decided that a colony should be established on the island to secure British territorial claims. Although this was the first formal European settlement it was the culmination of over a decade of random exploitation and plunder by whalers and sealers who had already established a pattern of maltreatment of the local Aboriginal population. It was common for sealers to enslave Aboriginal women and to use them for both sexual purposes and hunting.

Between March 1803 and June 1804 convicts, soldiers and free settlers arrived at Risdon Cove and Sullivans Cove on the Derwent River. The settlement was named Hobart Town. The early history of the settlement was characterised by extreme hardship and constant skirmishes with the local Aborigines.

Later in 1804 a settlement was established at George Town at the mouth of the Esk River. Two years later it moved inland to the present site of Launceston. It wasn't until 1812 that the independent settlements at Hobart and Launceston were brought together under a single administration.

In the early years of settlement free settlers were encouraged in spite of the difficulties presented by the land and the island's infant economy. By 1820 the island's European population was 5468 of whom 2588 had arrived as convicts.

The life of convicts transported to Van Diemen's Land was impossibly difficult. Those sent to Macquarie Harbour, on the island's west coast, were expected to row up to 20 miles a day from the penal camp at Sarah Island to the Gordon River where they felled huon pine for the construction of ships. At Port Arthur the line between 'convict labour' and 'slavery' blurred when convicts were used to power a huge 24-man treadmill—surely one of the most demeaning and arduous forms of punishment ever invented.

The most important work done by convict gangs in the early nineteenth century centred on the establishment of a series of elegant stone villages (including some particularly impressive bridges and churches) along the route from Hobart to Launceston. Today villages like Richmond and Ross bear witness to this work.

In 1825 Van Diemen's Land became a separate colony. The early governors—Arthur (1824–36), Franklin (1837–43), Eardley-Wilmot (1843–46) and Denison (1847–55)—struggled to manage a colony which was expanding rapidly. Thirteen thousand convicts arrived on the island between 1817 and 1830. Most were assigned to the new landowners.

During this period Aborigines were hunted and killed like animals. It is probable that some kind of undeclared warfare—more a series of skirmishes between settlers and Aborigines—broke out.

The island's fragile economy became a continuing nemesis. In the 1830s, when the economy was

Port Arthur in the 1880s.

relatively stable, settlers still had to grapple with high interest rates and a shortage of currency. A sudden boom in land prices in the late 1830s led to a depression in the 1840s which was exacerbated by too much spare convict labour.

The situation became so bad that Lieutenant-Governor Franklin was recalled to England in 1843 and his successor, Eardley-Wilmot, was confronted with horrendous economic problems as a result of the British government's refusal to pay for the police or the gaols.

Tasmanians have often looked for scapegoats. In the 1840s the island's economic problems were blamed on transportation. Although the economy began to improve in the latter part of the decade it was not enough to slow down a burgeoning anti-transportation movement lead by the preacher and historian, John West. The Governor of the time, William Thomas Denison, resisted the anti-transportation moves but by 1852 the island had a representative council and the British parliament agreed that transportation would cease the following year.

In spite of these changes (and a change of name from Van Diemen's Land to Tasmania in 1855) the island's economic woes persisted. The economy was almost continuously depressed from 1856 to 1872. Wages fell, crops failed and labourers left their jobs in droves to try their luck on the Victorian goldfields. The economy of the island was barely surviving on exports of whale oil and fruit.

Tasmania's saviour went by the unlikely name of 'Philosopher' Smith. For twenty-five years he had been prospecting along the island's west coast. In 1871 he discovered tin at Mount Bischoff and, although the west coast has some of the harshest weather conditions in Australia, the prospect of riches attracted men to the area where subsequently gold was found along the Pieman River, silver was found at Waratah, Zeehan, Dundas and Farrell, copper was mined at Mount Lyell and tin at Renison Bell.

In twenty years (1871–91) the island's population rose from 99 000 to 146 000. The mining boom flowed on to other industries. Fruit found a larger

Mount Wellington, near Hobart in the 1880s.

mainland market and wool established itself as the island's most significant export.

Unfortunately, this brief flurry of economic activity could not be sustained. World War I drew men away from the island and the short postwar boom was not accompanied by any significant increase in prosperity or population. The population was 218 316 in the census of 1921 and this had only increased to 227 000 by 1931.

Surprisingly, since World War II Tasmania's population has grown. In 1992 it was 471 118. Although the state still has high unemployment levels it has been seen by many people as an alternative to the increasing Americanisation and modernisation of the mainland centres.

The forces at work in contemporary Tasmania are complex and unusual. They seem to be the result of a conflict between deeply conservative rural communities and radical, free-thinking new settlers who advocate modern moral and social reforms.

This conflict can be seen in such contemporary issues as the environment—in the 1989 Federal elections five Tasmanian seats were won by Greens—and homosexual law reform.

'This is a confused and complex society in crisis,' Peter Hay, a political scientist at the University of Tasmania has observed. 'It isn't sure where it's going. It's had an uncomplicated modern history; it was sure of itself. Everyone believed in a small number of clichéd truths, but in the last twenty years that has all been thrown out the window.'

Due to the fear of terrorism in other parts of the world, Tasmania's tourist industry has benefitted. Tasmania boasts some of the most beautiful and rugged regions in the world as well as historic sites associated with Australia's very early years.

The sheer cliffs of Frenchmans Cap rise into the swirling mists of Tasmania's south-western nature-lands.

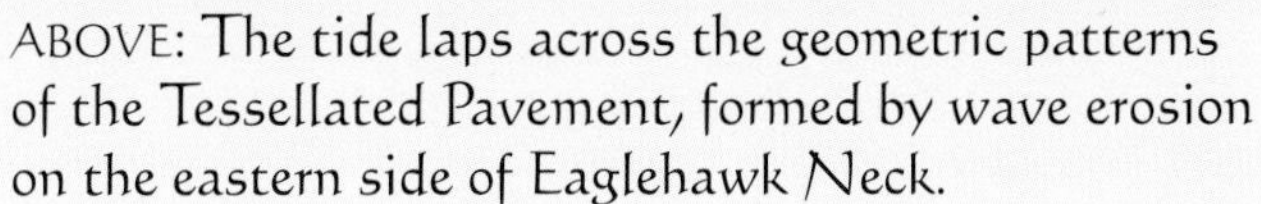

ABOVE: The tide laps across the geometric patterns of the Tessellated Pavement, formed by wave erosion on the eastern side of Eaglehawk Neck.

BELOW: Walkers enjoy the mossy forests and extensive tracks at Lake St Clair, one of the most famous hiking areas in Tasmania.

ABOVE: Enjoying breathtaking views across the blue waters of Lake Dove to the jagged silhouette of Cradle Mountain in the northern end of the magnificent Cradle Mountain-Lake St Clair National Park.

OPPOSITE: Rugged coastline at Sleepy Bay on the Freycinet Peninsula.

OVERLEAF: Lake Pedder, a clear glacial lake nestling among jagged peaks in the Southwest National Park, was flooded in 1972 as part of a hydroelectric scheme.

BELOW: The highlands of Tasmania are home to the Tasmanian Devil (Sarcophyllus harisii), Australia's largest marsupial predator.

ABOVE: One of Australia's most famous historic sites—the Port Arthur convict settlement. About 12 500 men and boys were transported here.

BELOW: Wrest Point Casino, Australia's first hotel/casino and Tasmania's most renowned venue for sophisticated nightlife.

OPPOSITE: Colourful open-air craft markets at Salamanca Place, Hobart, where fine examples of early merchant warehouses can be seen.

OVERLEAF: Hobart, seen here from the Mt Nelson lookout, is Australia's second oldest and most southerly city.

BELOW: A very heavy game of chess at Franklin Square, Hobart.

Schwarzkopf
NO PARKING
TASMANIAS UNIQUE TIMBERS

LEFT: Hobart is memorable for its deep-water harbour on the estuary of the Derwent River, its mellow early colonial sandstone buildings and the backdrop of majestic Mt Wellington.

OPPOSITE: New Norfolk, on the banks of the Derwent River, is a classified historic town nestled among English trees and hop fields.

BELOW: A suspension bridge straddles the South Esk River at Cataract Gorge, Launceston.

ABOVE: Tasmania's rivers provide great opportunities for exhilarating jet boat rides.

OPPOSITE: The quaint township of Stanley nestles under a massive rocky outcrop known as The Nut. Old whalers and sailing ships used to berth at the wharf here, nowadays the wharf handles crayfish and shark fishing fleets.

BELOW: Pennyfarthing races at the small unspoilt township of Evandale, where buildings date from as early as 1809.

BELOW: One of Launceston's best-known tourist attractions, the Penny Royal Watermill complex, which includes a museum, working cornmill and a windmill.

ABOVE: Winterscape in the Cradle Mountain–Lake St Clair National Park.

LEFT: Cascading falls and moss covered vegetation are features of the water-dominated south-west coast.

BELOW: Tasmania's majestic, untamed west coast is indented by wild rivers meeting the sea.

ABOVE: The Wilderness Seeker carries sightseers down the magnificent Gordon River in south-west Tasmania, one of the last great temperate wilderness areas in the world.

OPPOSITE: The dark cliffs of Cape Pillar and Tasman Island rise up from the deep blue of the Tasman Sea.

BELOW: Waves froth against the rocky coastline on Tasmania's west coast.

BELOW: Winter sports on the snowfields at Ben Lomond National Park in north-eastern Tasmania.

LEFT: Winter light on the War Memorial at Queenstown, an old mining town carved out of the surrounding mountains.

BELOW: Richmond Bridge, the oldest bridge in Australia, is one of the many attractions in the historic town of Richmond.

OPPOSITE, TOP: The lush countryside near Deloraine is used mainly for dairying and mixed farming.

OPPOSITE, BOTTOM: Picturesque Strahan, the only port on the rugged west coast of Tasmania.

HAMERS HOTEL

ABOVE: Autumn colours the hop fields at Bushy Park near New Norfolk.

OPPOSITE: Liffy Falls, near Deloraine, are a spectacular example of the many beautiful waterfalls found in the rainforests of Tasmania

BELOW: The largest lavender farm outside Europe is found at Nabowla, a farming township in north-east Tasmania.

BELOW: Surf, rock, spear and estuary fishing are all available at the popular holiday resort of Bicheno on the east coast.

King William Street, Adelaide, in the 1880s.

The Rotunda, Adelaide c. 1886.

The flag of South Australia (the Festival State).
This flag was adopted on 13 January 1904. The flag consists of a British Blue Ensign with the state badge sitting on a blue background. The badge displays a white-backed piping shrike (magpie) with wings outstretched on a yellow disc. The badge design is attributed to Robert Craig of the Adelaide School of Arts.

South Australia has adopted the well-known Sturt's desert pea (pictured opposite) as its floral emblem, the hairynosed wombat as its animal emblem, the piping shrike as its unofficial faunal emblem and the leafy sea-dragon as its marine emblem.

South Australia: The Heritage

by Bruce Elder

In 1627 the Dutch ship, Gulden Zeepaard, sailed along the southern coast of New Holland and reached the area around Ceduna in South Australia before turning back and making its way north to Batavia. This was the first recorded sighting of South Australia by Europeans.

The coastline remained unexplored until 1792 when the French explorer, Bruni d'Entrecasteaux, sailed up into the Great Australian Bight. He was followed in 1800 by Lieutenant James Grant and in 1802 by Matthew Flinders who, during his circumnavigation of Australia, chartered much of the future state's coastline. These explorers did little to encourage settlers to the area. Their reports of a difficult coastline with a dry, harsh hinterland were not designed to create a rush of interest. In fact, in 1804, a government survey ship sailed along the coast of Kangaroo Island and concluded that it was unsuitable for human habitation.

The eventual settlement of South Australia by Europeans was the result of an experiment in social engineering. In the early part of the nineteenth century, with people pouring into the overcrowded cities of England, social reform became increasingly important.

Against this background the tireless social reformer, Edward Gibbon Wakefield, developed a theory of systematic colonisation. He rejected the notion of colonies being a dumping ground for Britain's prison overflow and advanced a scheme where the money raised from the sale of crown land could be invested in the cost of shipping labourers to work on the newly privatised land. Here was a plan for the development of Australia which did not rely on convict labour.

In the early stages it seemed that bureaucracy would conspire to ensure that it failed. However, in May 1835 ten commissioners were appointed to oversee the sale of land in the new colony of South Australia. Before the colony could become a reality they needed to sell land to the value of £35 000. This was achieved in seven months.

In rapid succession Captain John Hindmarsh was appointed Governor of the new colony, William Light was appointed Surveyor-General, James Hurtle Fisher was appointed Resident Commissioner and eight ships sailed from England bound for the shores of South Australia.

By March 1837 William Light had surveyed the site of Adelaide and land had been allotted. It looked as though the colony would be an unqualified success. Livestock and settlers were pouring into South Australia and there was a sense of entrepreneurial enthusiasm in the air. Unfortunately most of the new settlers seemed more interested in land

Port Adelaide lighthouse in the 1880s.

speculation than in clearing land, growing crops and trying to make their allotments economically viable.

Acrimony between the Governor and Resident Commissioner resulted in their recall to England and the appointment of Colonel George Gawler to both positions. Gawler tried to control what was rapidly becoming an uncomfortable free-for-all. By 1840 there were 14 000 people in the colony and the government was effectively bankrupt. Money had been poorly spent, only 7500 labourers had been sent to the colony, and there were accusations of serious financial mismanagement.

By 1842 the British government had deemed the experiment a failure and South Australia had reverted to an ordinary Crown colony. In spite of this turnaround the experiment did eventually work. Two years later under the governorship of Captain George Grey, the colony had resolved its financial problems and the farmers (landowners who, in many instances, had been persuaded to go and work their land) were actually producing more wheat than the colony could use.

The colony's economic base expanded during the 1840s when silver was discovered near Adelaide and huge copper deposits were located near Kapunda. This mining activity, when added to the successes in the rural sector, attracted new immigrants and by 1850 the population of South Australia had grown to 64 000.

The discovery of gold the following year saw the colony's population drop by 25 per cent as men rushed to the goldfields. In a particularly astute move the colony's parliament passed the Bullion Act which offered a range of incentives to miners to return to South Australia with their wealth. So successful was the legislation (which offered high local prices for gold and regular gold escorts) that more than £2 million returned to Adelaide in two years.

The miners who returned wanted a more democratic political process and in the mid-1850s they successfully petitioned Britain to establish two elected houses of parliament to administer the colony. In this they reflected the political radicalism which was sweeping Australia at the time.

The result was a new constitution for South Australia which was widely regarded as the most forward-looking and democratic in the British Empire. Unfortunately the constitution was not accompanied by the establishment of political parties and, with independents dominating, the power base changed no fewer than thirty-seven times in the next thirty-three years.

The most important reform brought about during this volatile period was the establishment of the Torrens Title system of registering land. This piece of legislation, introduced by Sir Robert Torrens in 1858, eventually would be adopted throughout Australia.

By the 1860s the economic success of the goldrushes had given way to a period of economic hardship. In spite of this the state prospered. John McDouall Stuart became the first person to cross the continent from south to north. In the process he opened up valuable grazing lands in the north of the state. Huge copper reserves were found at Moonta. South Australia gained control of the Northern Territory in 1863 and the state's sheep and human populations nearly doubled in the decade. This prosperity and success continued until the depression of the 1880s.

The boom of the 1860s collapsed in the 1880s when the state's population growth slowed and

Onkaparinka and the Rock in the Adelaide Hills, South Australia, in the 1880s.

its agricultural productivity, hit by drought, was greatly reduced. This was to become a pattern for future decades. The problem was that so much of the state was marginal land. The slightest change in climatic or economic conditions had the consequence of decimating what had previously been valuable and economically viable.

As with the depression of the 1860s the state's economic fortunes were saved by the discovery of silver, lead and zinc at Broken Hill. Although the mine was in New South Wales the economic benefits flowed into South Australia where huge treatment works were constructed at Port Pirie, bringing work and prosperity to the area.

Combined with this windfall the state committed itself to expanding arable land through the use of superphosphates, to the clearing of marginal swamp land and to the establishment of communities along the Murray River.

During the 1890s the United Labor Party, a party formed by the local trade union movement, saw South Australia at the forefront of political reform. In 1891 free education was introduced and in 1894 the state granted full suffrage to women. The state also pioneered compulsory industrial arbitration during this period.

Economic prosperity was maintained through to the Great Depression. Iron ore was discovered to the west of Port Augusta at Iron Knob, a steelworks was built at Whyalla, the state's approach

Port Adelaide in 1840.

to land management and agricultural productivity was forward looking, and a strong secondary industry base was established during the first two decades of the twentieth century. After World War I the state actively settled returned soldiers on the Murray River floodplains and Adelaide grew rapidly.

The Depression decimated the state's economy. By 1931, 12 per cent of the state's population (24 per cent of its workforce) was unemployed. In 1933 the Labor government was defeated. It would not regain power until 1965. During this period the state's conservative forces, led from 1938 by Thomas (later Sir Thomas) Playford, would push the state's economy to new levels of success. This success was fuelled firstly by the manufacturing demands of World War II and secondly by the stable, and booming, economy which emerged in the postwar years. The list of achievements during this period is impressive. The Morgan–Whyalla pipeline was completed. The huge Whyalla steel-works and ship building yard were constructed. The Mannum pipeline bringing water from the Murray River to Adelaide was built. The city of Elizabeth, named after the Queen, was created in 1955. Oil refineries, cheap electricity, munitions factories and successful mining operations all helped to boost the state's economy. Although this was an enviable economic base it was still vulnerable to international forces.

Sir Thomas Playford's government was defeated by Labor in 1965. Playford had been state premier for twenty-eight years. It was the end of the state's political stability. The Labor Party ruled until 1968 when Steele Hall regained power for the Liberal Party. He was swept from office in 1970 when Don Dunstan became premier. In turn the Liberals regained power in 1979 under David Tonkin. They lost it in 1982 to John Bannon who, forced from office by a scandal involving the gross mismanagement of the state bank, was duly replaced by the Liberal Party in the early 1990s. Today Labor governs again.

These days South Australia has a reputation as a forward-looking, modern and innovative state. In the eyes of most Australians it is seen as the home of the country's wine industry and the Adelaide Festival, an arts festival of international repute.

Comfortable underground living at the opal-mining town of Coober Pedy where most of the population live in dugouts as protection from the severe temperatures.

ABOVE: Market day at Glenelg, Adelaide's most popular beach.

BELOW: 'Dingley Dell' home of the poet Adam Lindsay Gordon, now a museum in Port MacDonnell.

OPPOSITE: The Blessing of the Fleet at Port MacDonnell, home to the largest rock lobster fishing fleet in South Australia.

BELOW: Port Adelaide has many imposing buildings, a reminder of the port's heyday in the 1880s.

L91
CHATEAU YALDARA
Garden
BISTRO

AMP
AMP
Origin

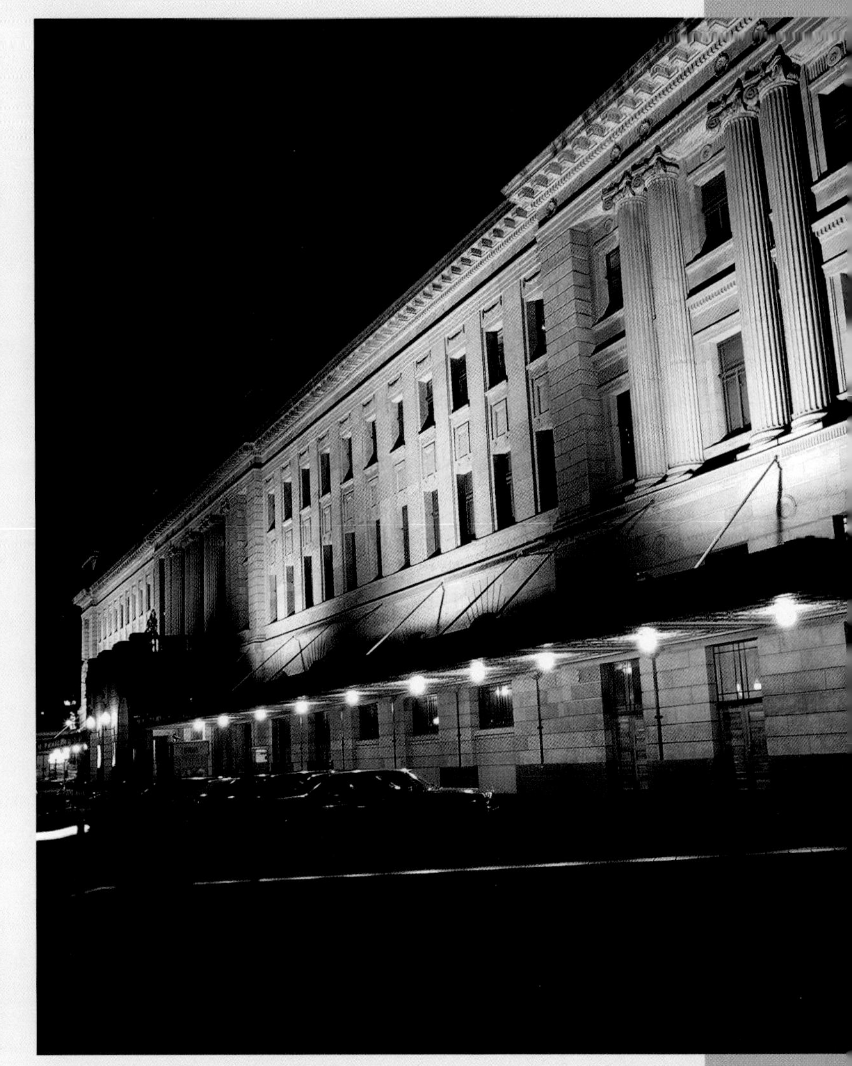

ABOVE: The Casino, Adelaide.

LEFT: The spacious, well-planned city of Adelaide is situated on the Torrens River on a narrow coastal plain between the blue waters of St Vincents Gulf and the rolling hills of the Mt Lofty Ranges. The Festival Theatre is in the foreground.

RIGHT: The picturesque Cape du Couedic lighthouse, one of the old landmarks in the Flinders Chase National Park on Kangaroo Island.

OPPOSITE: Twilight on the Torrens, Adelaide.

BELOW: The 197 metre deep Blue Lake near Mt Gambier changes from a dull grey to a vivid blue each November.

ABOVE: Council Chamber at Port Elliot, a quiet coastal town and the first port established on Encounter Bay.

ABOVE: Halfway mark at the small township of Kimba at the edge of South Australia's outback.

OPPOSITE: The Murray River flows through the Riverland district near Renmark. It is one of the most picturesque areas along the length of the river.

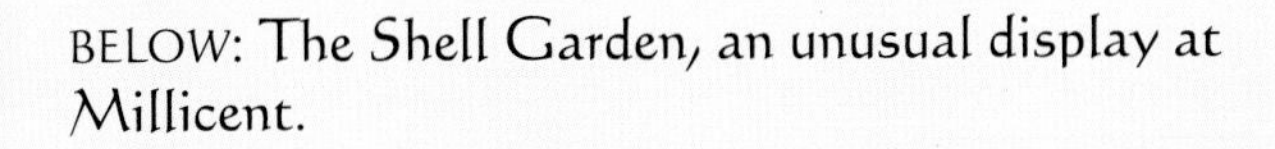

BELOW: The Shell Garden, an unusual display at Millicent.

BELOW: Wool is one of the main agricultural crops of South Australia.

CHATEAU YALDARA
Garden
BISTRO

ABOVE: Farm landscape in a valley near Quorn in the Flinders Ranges.

ABOVE: Many creeks wind their way through the valleys of the ancient Flinders Ranges.

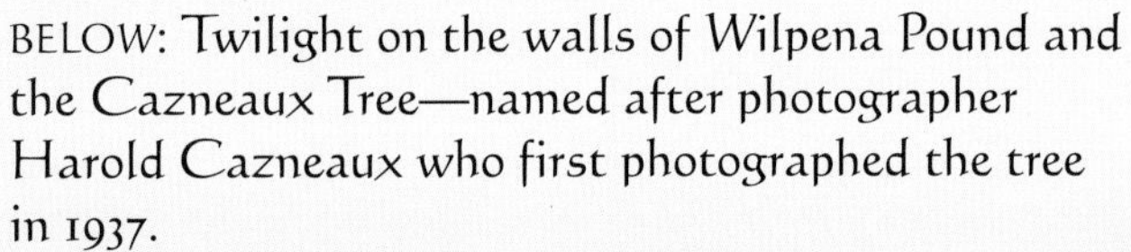

BELOW: Twilight on the walls of Wilpena Pound and the Cazneaux Tree—named after photographer Harold Cazneaux who first photographed the tree in 1937.

OPPOSITE: An unbroken wall of cliffs borders the edge of the Nullarbor Plain on the Great Australian Bight.

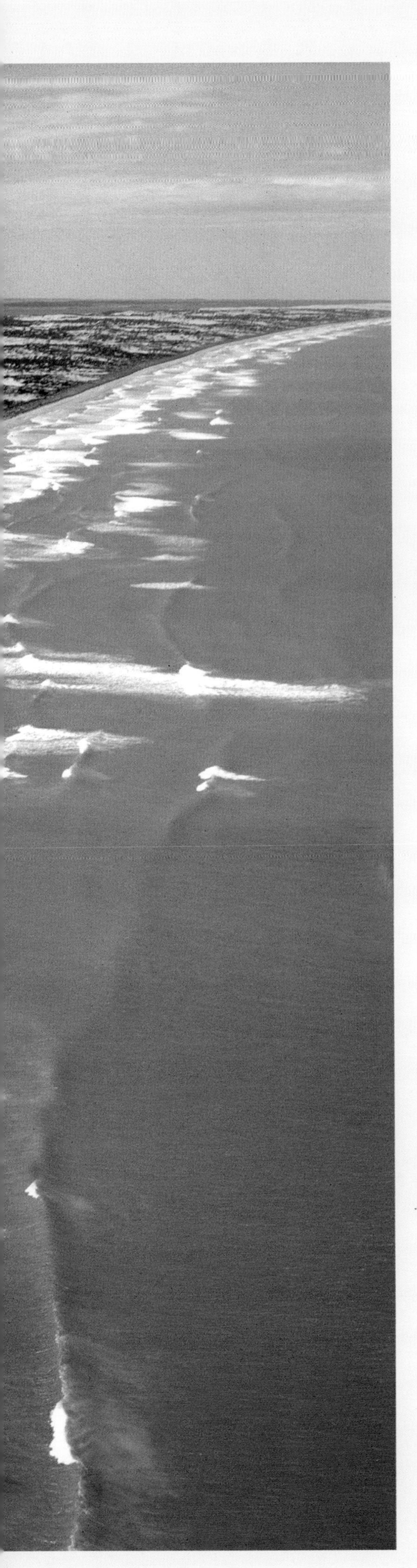

LEFT: A series of saltwater lagoons, fed by the waters of the Murray and divided from the sea by the massive white sandhills of the Younghusband Peninsula, the Coorong area is one of the last natural bird sanctuaries in Australia.

BELOW: The colourful Yarwondutta Rocks near Minnipa on the Eyre Peninsula.

ABOVE: Chateau Yaldara, near Lyndoch in the Barossa Valley, offers wine-tasting and sales.

ABOVE: Fascinating limestone formations at Kelly Hill Cave Conservation Park on Kangaroo Island.

OPPOSITE: Wilpena Pound in the Flinders Ranges, an immense elevated basin covering about 50 square kilometres and encircled by rock cliffs that rise more than 1000 metres from the surrounding plains.

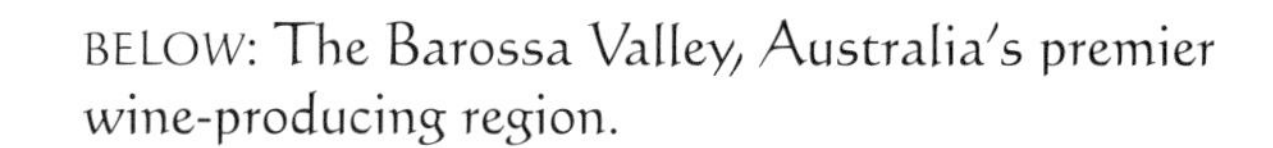

BELOW: The Barossa Valley, Australia's premier wine-producing region.

BELOW: The waters of the Torrens River froth through the Torrens Gorge near Adelaïde.

OPPOSITE: Pretty countryside seen from Norton Summit in the Mount Lofty Ranges behind Adelaide.

ABOVE: A National Park Ranger checks Australian sea lions at Seal Bay on Kangaroo Island.

BELOW: Early settlers' well in the South Australian outback near Marree.

ABOVE: In the Flinders Ranges, rich vegetation contrasts with stony rock faces at Brachina Gorge.

OPPOSITE: The late afternoon light on sand dunes near Merty Merty reveals the dramatic patterns made by the prevailing winds.

LEFT: The Pitchi Ritchi steam locomotive takes passengers on a round trip from Quorn, through the Pitchi Ritchi Pass.

OPPOSITE: The Sir Joseph Banks Group of Islands Conservation Park, off Tumby Bay on the east coast of the Eyre Peninsula.

BELOW: St Peter's Cathedral, Adelaide, one of Australia's finest cathedrals.

BELOW: South Australia is both the nation's wine capital and her festival state—here the two combine at the biennial Barossa Valley Vintage Festival, a thanksgiving celebration for a successful harvest.

ABOVE: The 'Remarkable Rocks' in Flinders Chase National Park on Kangaroo Island.

OPPOSITE: The remains of the wreck of the Ethel at Ethel Beach in Innes National Park.

Wild Dog Hill in the Whyalla Conservation Park in the heart of iron-ore mining country.

Many species of eucalypts, including the yellow gum, sugar gum and red river gum, are found in the Telowie Gorge Conservation Park as well as a spectacular springtime wattle display on the valley floor. The rugged landscape is also home to a community of rare yellow-footed wallabies.

Driftwood floats in the shallows in Coorong National Park. The 50 000 hectare park conserves a coastal dune system, lagoons, wetlands and coastal vegetation. It has been included on the list of 'Wetlands of International Importance'. It is also an important cultural site with evidence of thousands of years of Aboriginal occupation.

Tall red cliffs, gums and pines make up the spectacular scenery at Telowie Gorge Conservation Park.

Shearing.

Above: Horwick Street Perth, in the 1880s.

Below: Seizing a calf.

The flag of Western Australia (the State of Excitement).
This flag was adopted in 1953. The flag consists of a British Blue Ensign with the state badge sitting on a blue background. The badge displays a native black swan on a yellow disc with the swan swimming towards the flagpole. A variant to this design renders the swan more artistically and includes water ripples.

Western Australia has adopted the the Black Swan as its faunal emblem (pictured opposite), the numbat as its animal emblem and the red and green kangaroo paw as its floral emblem. No official marine emblem has been adopted.

Western Australia: The Heritage

by Bruce Elder

Although Western Australia covers nearly one-third of the Australian continent (it is 2 525 500 square kilometres) most of it is harsh, uninhabitable desert. In spite of its vast size Western Australia has a population of only 1 662 777 of whom 1.2 million live in Perth. Its economy is driven by mining, wool and wheat and yet only 15 per cent of the state's population live in rural areas.

The history of the state, in many ways, has been a continuous battle against the harshness of the vast deserts. So difficult is life beyond the narrow southern coastal strip that, in recent times, both Aborigines and white Australians have died of dehydration and exhaustion when they have lost their way or when their motor cars have broken down.

When, in 1699, William Dampier sailed down the coast of Western Australia, he noted the lack of water. His description of Shark Bay in *A Voyage to New Holland* expresses his frustration 'Twas the 7th of August when we came into Shark's Bay; in which we Anchor'd at three several Places, and stay'd at the first of them (on the W. side of the Bay) till the 11th. During which time we searched about, as I said, for fresh Water, digging Wells, but to no purpose.'

Australia's first inhabitants probably arrived on the coast of north-west Western Australia some 50 000 years ago. Over the next 20 000 years they slowly moved southward and eastward across the landmass. Certainly Aborigines were well established throughout Western Australia by the time the Dutch ships started reaching the coast in the early seventeenth century. In fact there is considerable evidence that the obvious poverty of the coastal Aborigines, who were trying to eke out a living from near-desert, did much to discourage serious exploration of the coast.

After Henderik Brouwer and Dirk Hartog, the Dutch sailor Willem de Vlamingh reached the island in 1697 and, finding Hartog's pewter plate still in its original position, removed it and replaced it with another. The original was returned to Holland where it still is kept in the Rijksmuseum.

De Vlamingh's replacement plate had an even less interesting inscription than Hartog's. After getting the date wrong he listed all the important sailors on the voyage and concluded with 'Our fleet set sail from here to continue exploring the Southern Land, on the way to Batavia.'

In 1818 the French explorer Louis de Freycinet, while exploring the coast, came across de Vlamingh's plate and removed it to France. The plate was eventually returned to Australia in 1947

Packing wool in the 1880s.

and is currently housed in the Maritime Museum in Fremantle.

In the early nineteenth century the British became concerned about the possibility of a French colony being established on the coast of Western Australia and thus, in 1826, the New South Wales Governor Ralph Darling was instructed to establish a colony at King George Sound with a view to establishing a permanent penal colony there. The 'penal colony' (24 convicts and a detachment of soldiers) was short-lived. By 1831 it had closed and a new, and more permanent, colony had been established on the Swan River 500 kilometres to the north.

The founding father of modern Western Australia was Captain James Stirling who, in 1827, explored the Swan River area in the HMS Success. As a result of his explorations attempts to establish a new colony in the west were renewed and on 2 May 1829 Captain Charles Fremantle claimed Western Australia for Britain. A month later a party of free settlers, accompanied by free workers (the plan was to establish the colony without convict labour) arrived under the control of Captain Sterling and a colony was established near the mouth of the Swan River.

By 1831 the population of the colony had reached 1500 but the difficulties of clearing the land and growing crops were so great that by 1850 the population had only increased to 5886. This population settled around the south-western coastline at Bunbury, Augusta and Albany and slowly moved inland looking for pastures for their flocks, cutting down the hardwoods and grubbing out sandalwood for export to Asia.

In spite of this relative success the colony could not resist the temptation of convict labour and on 1 June 1850 the first boatload of convicts arrived. Western Australia was becoming a convict state at a time when the eastern states, largely due to the goldrushes, were abandoning convict labour. Between 1850 and 1868, when transportation stopped, a total of 9718 convicts arrived. Their effect on the colony's economy was considerable and by 1869 the population had increased to 22 915.

The harshness of the climate and the marginal nature of the land ensured that Western Australia would never be densely populated. Even Perth, which was to grow into a particularly beautiful modern city, struggled with its population. By 1849, there were 1148 living in the city and by 1891 this had only grown to 8447. Even in 1911 it was just a medium-sized country town with a population of 31 300. The arrival of the Trans-Australian Railway in 1917 and the early success of the gold-mining towns pushed the population to 272 528 in 1947 and the subsequent immigration from Britain meant that by 1990, there were 1 193 100 people living in Perth and its suburbs. In this sense it is probably the only Australian capital city which is almost totally dependent on the economic well-being of the state.

In his novel City of Men, Gavin Casey astutely observes: 'When the crop fails the city fails. Townies who ask how the wheat-belt is looking aren't just making conversation. They want to know. It's a wheat-growing city, if you can understand the term. It doesn't make anything. It just buys and sells things, and the only places to which it can sell anything except the wheat and wool and gold are the goldfields, the wheat-belt and the grazing areas.'

Until the 1870s the economy of the state was

Mustering sheep in the 1880s.

based on wheat, meat and wool. The early explorers opened up the inland but they were not followed by eager developers because all they found was desert. Major Peter Egerton Warburton made the perilous journey from Alice Springs to the Western Australian coast. A. C. and F. T. Gregory in the 1840s and 1850s carried out extensive explorations along the continent's western coastline and hinterland. Ernest Giles twice traversed the Gibson Desert.

The real change in the state's fortunes occurred in the 1880s when gold was discovered and prospectors by the tens of thousands swarmed across the land in a desperate attempt to discover new goldfields. Paddy Hannan's discovery at Kalgoorlie, and the early discoveries at Coolgardie, sparked true gold fever.

In 1891 the rush to the Murchison goldfields began when Tom Cue discovered gold at the town which now bears his name. In the years that followed dozens of gold towns—Day Dawn, Meekatharra, Nannine, Peak Hill, Garden Gully, Dead Finish, Pinnicles, Austin Island and Austin Mainland—grew up only to die when the seams were exhausted and the gold fever moved on.

As a result of this sudden influx of miners, and the wealth which they brought with them, the state was granted responsible government in 1890.

The wealth generated from gold soon disappeared and by the early years of the twentieth century the economy was once again dependent on wool and wheat. This dependency meant that a dramatic fall in wool and wheat prices in the late 1920s to early 1930s saw the state's economy collapse. It was not to

recover until after World War II when the Federal government's postwar immigration policy saw a huge influx of migrants, nearly all of them from Britain, in the period 1947 to 1970.

In the early 1980s the state boasted the remarkable population profile of having 1.3 million people of whom 72 per cent were native-born Australians and 15 per cent were British-born immigrants.

Symbolic of these new immigrants was Alan Bond who, along with Robert Holmes à Court, Laurie Connell, Brian Burke, and a large number of high-flying entrepreneurs, put Western Australia very firmly back on the Australian map during the 1980s.

Bond was symptomatic of the times—high profile and prepared to do anything to draw attention to the state. His coup was the winning of the elusive America's Cup. He had four attempts at the Cup before he was successful.

Bond was matched for audacity by Robert Holmes à Court whose Bell Group made a bid for Australia's biggest company, BHP. The bid was repulsed but not before Holmes à Court made it clear that he had $2.5 billion credit available for future takeovers.

In tandem with these dealings the premier, Brian Burke, did everything in his power to nurture the entrepreneurs. Such was the government's involvement that the term 'WA Inc' was coined to describe its entrepreneurial enthusiasm.

By the mid-1980s Western Australia was the land of opportunity. It was the state where everyone could get rich quickly. However, the stockmarket crash of 1987 put an end to all these dreams. Western Australia is still a gigantic and very successful mineral bin with huge deposits of iron ore, gold and diamonds but the entrepreneurs have all fallen from grace. Following this, for a time, the state retreated into a new conservatism and nurtured a sense of separateness which looked with disdain on the decadent lifestyle of those who lived on the continent's east coast. This is changing now and recently the people elected another Labor Party, this time led by Geoff Gallop and this has since proved to be popular with most of the electorate.

An aboriginal camp in the 1880s.

A welcome creek bed west of Carnegie Homestead. Here in the centre of Western Australia, the Gunbarrel Highway degenrates into harsh gravel tracks with numerous creek crossings.

OVERLEAF: Perth, the capital of Western Australia, is situated on the banks of the clear blue Swan River.

CITIBANK
CIC

AMP
ANZ

ABOVE: Burswood Resort Casino, Perth.

OPPOSITE, TOP: St Francis Xavier Cathedral, Geraldton.

OPPOSITE, BOTTOM LEFT: Hay Street Mall, in the centre of Perth's shopping district.

OPPOSITE, BOTTOM RIGHT: New Norcia Cathedral. This settlement had its origins in a mission established by Spanish Benedictine monks in 1846.

ROSENDORFF'S

ABOVE: Gardens at the resort town of Yanchep, north of Perth.

RIGHT: The spring-flowering Albany cat's paw (Anigozanthos preissi) is native to the south-western part of the state.

OPPOSITE: A carpet of wildflowers sets the countryside south of Perth ablaze every spring.

OPPOSITE, TOP: Carnarvon's prawn fleet lines up at the jetty.

OPPOSITE, BOTTOM LEFT: Goldrush relics are displayed at the Goldfields Museum in Coolgardie, one of the best known ghost towns in Australia.

OPPOSITE, BOTTOM RIGHT: Sand patterns on Babbage Island, Carnarvon.

ABOVE: Reflections at the former goldmining town of Mount Magnet.

BELOW, LEFT: Intricate formations decorate Lake Cave in the Leeuwin-Naturaliste National Park.

BELOW: Lake Argyle, created by the Ord River Dam, is ideal for boating and fishing.

ABOVE: Marble Bar, reputedly the hottest place in Australia, takes its name from the bar of red-coloured jasper which crosses the Coongnan River.

OPPOSITE: Palm trees frame Echidna Gorge in the Bungle Bungle National Park.

ABOVE: Ruins of the Old Telegraph Station at Eucla, once one of the busiest in Australia, are gradually being covered by sand.

BELOW: The rugged peaks of the Stirling Range rise abruptly above countryside rich in native vegetation.

ABOVE: The boiling white foam of the Southern Ocean pounds against jagged rock formations at East Mylies Beach at Fitzgerald River National Park.

BELOW: The steep-sided multi-coloured walls of Geikie Gorge rise some 60 metres above the water.

OPPOSITE: White sandy bays and granite headlands at Thistle Cove in the Cape Le Grand National Park near Esperance.

ABOVE: Cheynes Beach Whaling Station Museum near Albany. The whaling fleet once based here used to harpoon about 700 whales per year.

BELOW: Stopover at the National Hotel in the tiny settlement of Sandstone off the Great Northern Highway.

ABOVE: Sunset over the Gibson Desert.

OPPOSITE: Solitude at Cable Beach, Broome.

LEFT: Signpost on the Western Australia/South Australia border.

OPPOSITE: Hamersley Gorge, in the heart of Australia's great western mountain chain.

BELOW: Pearl luggers and fishing boats at Streeters Wharf, Broome.

ABOVE: The Hamersley Range stretches more than 300 kilometres through the mineral-rich Pilbara region.

BELOW: Intrepid travellers on the Gunbarrel Highway in the Gibson Desert.

ABOVE: Deep River flows into the Nornalup inlet, a broad expanse of water surrounded by the Walpole-Nornalup National Park.

BELOW: Estimated to be 2700 million years old, the remarkable 15 metre high Wave Rock in Hyden has been naturally sculpted out of granite.

ABOVE: The Pinnacle Desert, unusual limestone rock formations in the Nambung National Park.

OPPOSITE: Rugged coloured hills surround the Ord River near Kununurra, Aboriginal for 'big water'.

ABOVE: Shot Hole Canyon, near Exmouth in the arid Pilbara region, one of the most heavily mineralised areas in the world.

BELOW: One of the many colourful restaurants at Fremantle, the largest port in the state.

ABOVE: Hawks Head Lookout affords magnificent views over the wild landscape of Kalbarri National Park, encompassing the lower reaches of the Murchison River.

OPPOSITE: Yardie Creek, imprisoned between vertical cliffs, is the only permanent water in the rugged Cape Range National Park.

Palmerston from Fort Hill in the 1880s. The modern city of Darwin was developed on this site.

Rounding up a straggler.

The flag of the Northern Territory (Outback Australia).
This flag was adopted on 1 July 1978, though the Northern Territory was founded as a Federal Territory on 1 January 1811. The flag uses th Territorian colours, the floral emblem and the Southern Cross and w designed by the well-known Victorian illustrator Robert Ingpen.

The Northern Territory has adopted Sturt's desert pea as its floral emblem, the red kangaroo as its animal emblem (pictured opposite) a the wedge-tailed eagle as its faunal emblem. No official marine embl has been adopted.

Northern Territory: The Heritage

by Bruce Elder

The Northern Territory of Australia is large in area and small in population. Covering 1 346 200 square kilometres (only Western Australia and Queensland are larger), it is larger than France, Germany and the United Kingdom combined. Yet the territory's population in 1992 was only 168 643. It is a vast wilderness of desert, scrub, savanna grassland and mangrove swamps. Its economy is driven by mining, cattle and tourism. It is, in a very real sense, Australia's last frontier.

There is little doubt that the territory's 6200 kilometre coastline has been the site of most of the continent's significant sightings and arrivals. Available evidence suggests that some 50 000 years ago the ancestors of Aborigines arrived in the Northern Territory travelling overland from the north.

It is probable that the first non-Aborigine to sight the coast was the Chinese explorer Cheng Ho, who in the early years of the fifteenth century ventured into the Indian Ocean. It is quite likely that a statue found near the present-day site of Darwin in 1879 was left by Cheng Ho.

The first confirmed European contact with Australia occurred when Willem Janszoon explored Cape York in 1606. Seventeen years later Jan Carstensz, commanding the Dutch East India ships the Pera and Arnhem sailing east from the trading port of Batavia, explored the south coast of New Guinea and discovered and named the Gulf of Carpentaria and Arnhem Land.

The entire coastline was explored and chartered by Abel Tasman in 1644 and in 1803, during his circumnavigation of Australia, Matthew Flinders chartered the coast although he did not recognise Melville Island as being separate from the mainland. That was left to Phillip Parker King in 1818.

King found to his surprise that the Aborigines knew some Portuguese words suggesting that they had made contact with Portuguese sailors and that a Portuguese ship had possibly been wrecked nearby. King named the island after Viscount Melville.

Early attempts to settle the coast of the Northern Territory can best be described as tragic disasters. The British, fearing that the explorations of Frenchmen like Nicolas Baudin would lead to the establishment of a French colony, decided that it was necessary to establish a fort or an outpost on the coast.

The first attempt occurred in 1824 when the British government sent three vessels, under the leadership of Captain J. J. G. Bremer. The ships arrived at Port Essington and, determined to lay claim to the area, he declared that the north coast of Australia from 129° to 135° east was a British colony.

Cooper Creek.

On 26 September 1824 the party landed at King Cove and over the next month a settlement was built. On 21 October it was named Fort Dundas.

There was no reason to settle the area, beyond a vague notion that the French or Dutch may lay claim to the region. This became very obvious when sickness, attacks from the local Aborigines and pirates, and dissension over policies caused pressures in the community. By 1826 the post was being wound down and it was officially closed in 1829.

In 1826, after unsatisfactory reports of the settlement at Fort Dundas had filtered through to the Colonial Office in London, it was decided to set up a second military outpost at Raffles Bay. The outpost was to be known as Fort Wellington. The 'settlers' consisted of some convicts and some members of the 39th Regiment. They arrived at Raffles Bay on 17 June 1827.

The settlement suffered the inevitable problems of disease, pestilence, tropical lethargy, attacks from unfriendly Aborigines, and isolation. In 1828, with the arrival of Collet Barker, it looked as though the settlement might succeed. Barker established good relations with the Aborigines and started encouraging settlement from the East Indies. However the settlement was closed down in 1829.

Port Essington was the third attempt to settle the northern coastline. Because the settlement lasted for over a decade, and because it was the site of Ludwig Leichhardt's greatest triumph, it is perhaps more widely known than the other less successful attempts at Raffles Bay and Fort Dundas.

Port Essington was actually chosen as the site of the first settlement but when the settlement party arrived in 1824 they found that there was no fresh water and so, after three days, they moved to Fort Dundas.

On 26 October 1838 Captain J. J. Gordon Bremer (who, by this time, must have been convinced that he was really out of luck when it came to leading expeditions) arrived at Port Essington. It was a military outpost and for the next eleven years was manned almost exclusively by Royal Marines. The population never exceeded seventy-eight and the conditions were harsh.

In June 1839 Bremer had the good fortune to be posted to China to be part of the British forces during the Canton uprising. He never returned to the settlement which was smitten with fever and

the problems which had beset the other settlements in the area. The settlement was abandoned in 1849 and it wasn't until twenty years later that the successful settlement at Palmerston (the modern-day site of Darwin) was established.

It is worth remembering that Thomas Huxley passed through the settlement just before it closed down in 1849 and left a graphic description of the sheer awfulness of Port Essington describing it as 'the most wretched, the climate the most unhealthy, the human beings the most uncomfortable and houses in a condition most decayed and rotten.'

An early station homestead.

The history of permanent white settlement in the territory really started in 1861–62 when John McDouall Stuart, after two previously unsuccessful attempts, crossed the country from south to north. This was much more than just a successful expedition. The subsequent route for the Overland Telegraph Line was worked out by using Stuart's maps and journals. In turn the repeater stations which were established at Port Darwin, Yam Creek (Pine Creek), Daly Waters, Powells Creek, Tennant Creek, Barrow Creek, Alice Springs and Charlotte Waters along the Overland Telegraph route, became the first communities in the Territory.

The pastoralists compounded this by using the Telegraph Line as a stock route. To improve the water supply along the track bores were sunk and often where these bores were sunk a small community developed.

In the wake of all these people moving into the Territory it was inevitable that certain minerals were discovered and these mineral deposits also produced settlements.

Although John McDouall Stuart had passed through the Barkly Tablelands in 1862, the area's first explorers were Ludwig Leichhardt, who journeyed overland from Queensland in 1844, and Augustus Gregory who trekked south and east from the Victoria River in 1855. It was partly as a result of the rather exaggerated reports of Leichhardt and Gregory that the area was settled soon after the Overland Telegraph Line was built. Both explorers had returned with glowing reports of the grazing potential and this was enough to encourage adventurers to overland cattle into the area in the hope of making a quick fortune.

In 1863 the entire Northern Territory was annexed to South Australia and on 28 June 1864 Boyle Travers Finniss established a fourth coastal colony at Escape Cliffs. Like all the previous attempts it failed. It was abandoned two and a half years later.

The determination to settle the Territory remained undiminished. In 1869 George Goyder, the Surveyor-General of South Australia, arrived at Port Darwin. By 23 February he had surveyed the site of Darwin which was to be known as Palmerston. The timing was right. The Overland Telegraph had opened up the inland and by 1874 Palmerston had a population of 600 whites and 180 Chinese and Malays. The town had its own newspaper and there were eleven stores.

By the 1880s the northern coast was sparsely settled but, like so much of the Territory, all that was required was a good drought to drive even the

most committed pastoralist back to the milder and easier climates of the southern states.

The Barkly Tablelands to the south of Darwin were opened up by the famous stockman Nat Buchanan who travelled from Rocklands Station in Queensland across the tablelands to the Overland Telegraph Line in 1877. The trip was not very successful because by the time Buchanan arrived at the Telegraph Line speculators had already claimed, sight unseen, most of the land on the tablelands. The resulting invasion of sheep, which were totally unsuited to the ecology of the area, resulted in surveys being carried out in 1879 to determine ownership. By 1884 there were over 100 000 sheep in the area. In the 1890s the area became legendary as the great herds of beef cattle were driven across the semi–desert areas from the fertile Kimberleys into north Queensland.

During the war, with the aid of US funds, the Barkly Highway was built from just north of Tennant Creek across to Cloncurry via Mount Isa. It was subsequently upgraded so that today it is the main artery for all transportation through the area.

Independence for the Territory came slowly. In 1890 it elected two members to the South Australian House of Assembly and, with federation, the territory became part of the huge electorate of Grey.

In 1911 the Commonwealth government took over the administration of the territory. It was around this time that Palmerston became known as Darwin.

The Northern Territory probably changed from being perceived as a wild, tropical outpost to being an integral part of Australia during World War II. Fears of a possible Japanese invasion occurred shortly after the attack on Pearl Harbor in December 1941. Women and children were evacuated from Darwin and early in 1942 a number of American troops joined Australian forces. On 19 February 1942, 188 Japanese aircraft attacked Darwin. The official casualties numbered 243 dead and approximately 350 wounded.

Between 19 February 1942 and 12 November 1943, Darwin sustained 64 air attacks resulting in 261 deaths and 410 injured. It was impossible for people in the rest of Australia to pretend that the Northern Territory was a distant outpost. If Darwin was being attacked, Australia was being attacked.

After the war the Commonwealth government drew up plans to redevelop Darwin. The rebuilding of the city started in the early 1950s and by the mid-1970s it was expanding rapidly. This progress was halted on Christmas Day 1974 when Cyclone Tracy destroyed 90 per cent of the buildings and killed fifty people. The rebuilding of Darwin for the second time started at the end of 1975 and was completed in 1978. On 1 July 1978 the Territory was granted full self-government. For many years a Liberal-National coalition ruled with little opposition but following severe criticism for continuing its mandatory sentencing legislation for aboriginal law breakers, the Labor Party was elected. One of the new party's first pieces of legislation was to end mandatory sentencing.

Today the Territory has become one of Australia's premier tourist destinations. The beauties of the Kakadu National Park (which is now part of the World Heritage listings), the magic of Uluru and the dry, dramatic scenery around Alice Springs, attract vast numbers of visitors to the region. The population may still be small but the attractions are considerable.

ABOVE: Government House, Darwin, dates from 1870.

LEFT: One of Darwin's most historic hotels, The Old Victoria, has been restored and made into a modern shopping complex.

The relaxed city of Darwin, despite extensive damage from Cyclone Tracy in 1974, has grown in prosperity, based largely on the mineral wealth of the Northern Territory.

ABOVE: Watering hole at the tiny settlement of Daly Waters at the junction of the Stuart and Carpentaria Highways.

BELOW: The Mission Church at Daly River, a small township and Aboriginal Reserve on Joseph Bonaparte Gulf.

OPPOSITE: The Macdonnell Ranges curve in a great arc of parallel ridges across the very heart of Australia.

ABOVE: The bakery at the settlement of Pine Creek, originally a goldmining centre.

OPPOSITE: Twilight at Alice Springs in the heart of the Red Centre, almost 1000 kilometres from the nearest capital city.

LEFT: Sculptures by William Ricketts at Pitchi Ritchi open-air pioneer museum and bird and flower sanctuary at Alice Springs.

ALICE SPRINGS
WEST END
RAILWAYS CLUB
ALICE SPRINGS RAILWAYS CLUB
Kulgera
S.A. Border
Tennant Creek
Darwin

ABOVE: Waterlilies float on Majela Creek in the magnificent Kakadu National Park in the remote tropical north.

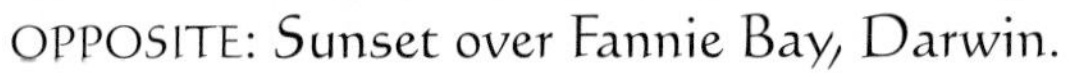

OPPOSITE: Sunset over Fannie Bay, Darwin.

BELOW: Kakadu National Park contains the most outstanding concentration of Aboriginal rock art in Australia.

BELOW: Dramatic rock patterns and formations, carved by ancient waterways, are a feature of King's Canyon National Park.

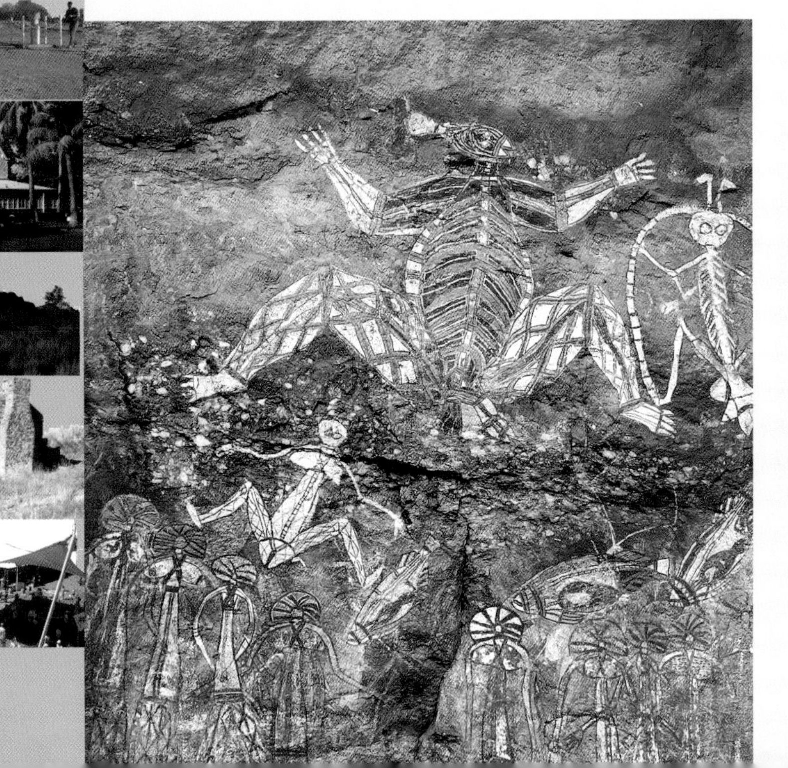

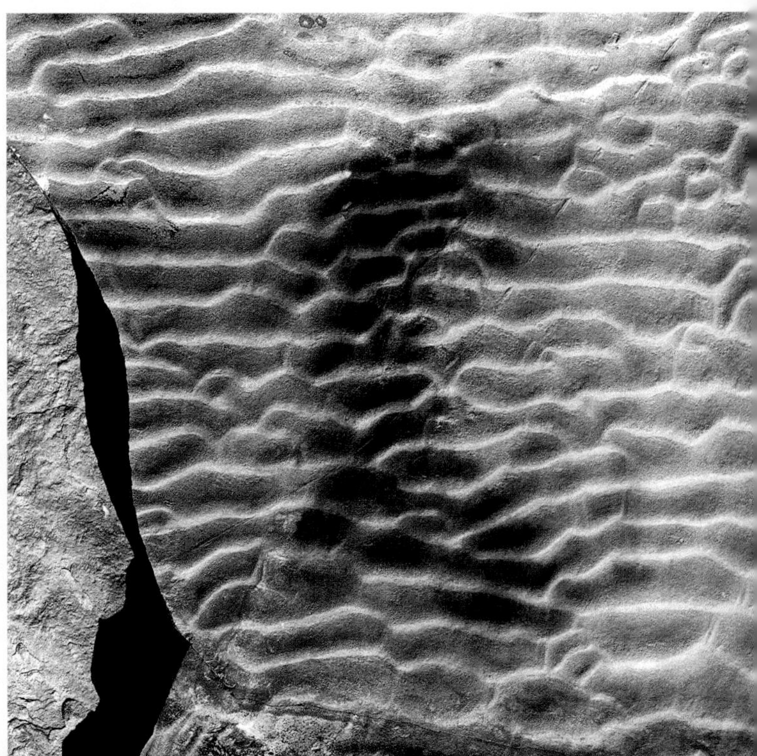

ABOVE: Heat rises and dust swirls at the outback cattle property of Mt Ebenezer near Alice Springs.

OPPOSITE: Obiri Rock in Kakadu National Park is a remnant of the original plateau, now cut back by the East Alligator River.

BELOW: Huge road trains are a familiar sight in the Outback areas of the Northern Territory.

ABOVE: The colours of Glen Helen Gorge, west of Alice Springs, have been captured by Aboriginal artist Albert Namatjira, and are today an inspiration to photographers.

OPPOSITE: Apart from a couple of large waterholes Ormiston Creek shrinks to scattered shallow puddles in the dry season, bordered by the dark red rocks of Ormiston Gorge.

ABOVE: Katatjuta—the Olgas—rise steeply from the desert in the Red Centre. The thirty domes are separated by narrow vertical chasms and the highest point is 450 metres above the plain.

OPPOSITE: White-trunked river gums contrast with dark red rock walls at Ellery Gorge in the Macdonnell Ranges, west of Alice Springs.

The huge sandstone Chambers Pillar, south of Alice Springs, catches the last rays of sunlight to glow above the surrounding countryside. Many early explorers have carved their names on this monolith.

ABOVE: A scene in the west MacDonnell Ranges.

LEFT: N'Dhala Gorge in the N'Dhala Gorge National Park. This shady gorge contains a wide range of rock carvings and paintings including over 6000 individual petroglyphs (prehistoric carvings).

BELOW: Tourists take a boat trip down the Katherine River to enjoy some of Australia's most spectacular gorge country.

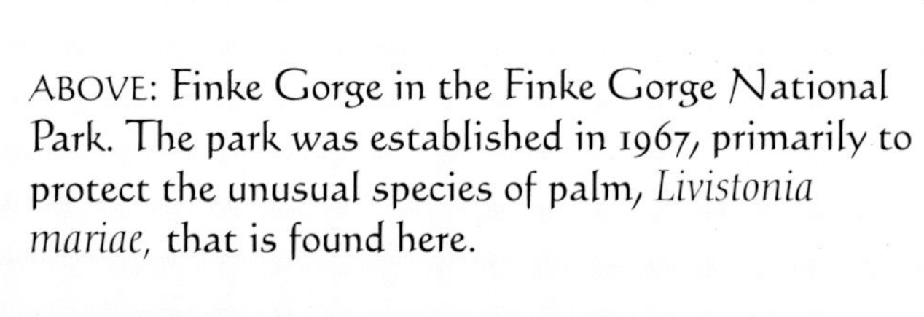

ABOVE: Finke Gorge in the Finke Gorge National Park. The park was established in 1967, primarily to protect the unusual species of palm, *Livistonia mariae,* that is found here.

RIGHT: Treescape in the Simpson Desert.

OPPOSITE: Magnificent galleries of Aboriginal rock paintings can be seen at Nourlangie Rock and other parts of Kakadu National Park. The aboriginal paintings of Kakadu and adjoining parts of western Arnhem Land are among the most outstanding in Australia. More than 300 major locations of paintings are recorded, some of which are galleries with friezes of paintings extending for up to 50 metres.

Cunningham's Gap

Brisbane Botanic Gardens in the 1880s.

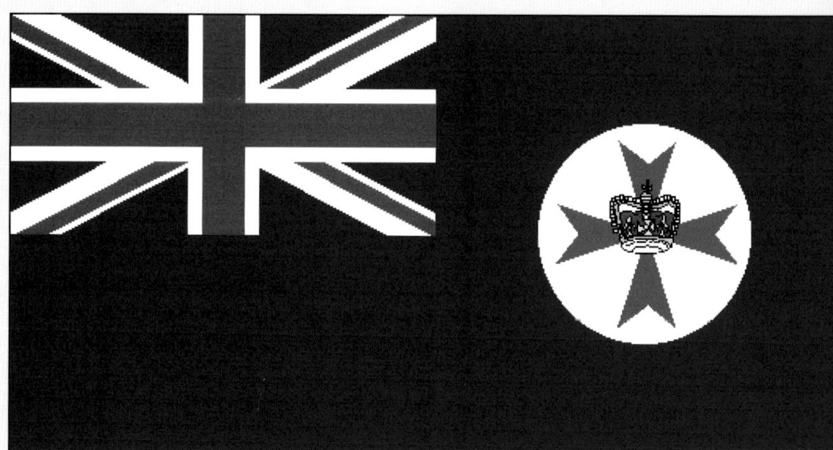

The flag of Queensland (The Sunshine State).
This flag was adopted 1876 and was designed by the Colonial Secretary and Treasurer of the time William Hemnant. The flag is a British Blue Ensign defaced with a St Edward's Crown in the centre of the cross on a white disc.

Queensland has adopted the Cooktown Orchid as its floral emblem (pictured opposite), the Koala as its animal emblem and the brolga as its faunal emblem. No official marine emblem has been adopted.

Queensland: The Heritage

by Bruce Elder

It is likely that the first contact with the Queensland coast made by Europeans occurred in 1606 when Captain Luis Vaez de Torres sailed south-west from the New Hebrides and probably came close to the reef near Cape York. The following year the Dutch sailor Willem Jansz made the first confirmed contact with the reefs in the Cape York area and in 1768 Bougainville heard the sound of waves crashing on the reef when he sailed as far south as the present site of Cooktown.

The first significant European contact occurred in 1770 when Captain James Cook sailed up the east coast of Australia charting and naming significant landmarks as he went. He saw Aborigines on the shore but made no attempt to explore the hinterland. Trying to chart his way through the Great Barrier Reef proved impossible and, as a result of the reef, Cook ran aground and was forced to drag his boat up for repairs in the estuary of the Endeavour River at the present-day site of Cooktown.

In 1799 Matthew Flinders sailed up the coast charting it as he went. He discovered rivers and bays which Cook's fairly superficial exploration had overlooked.

The reef was explored and surveyed between 1802 and 1850 by a variety of well-known adventurers and explorers amongst whom the most notable were Flinders, Philip King (1815) and Owen Stanley (1848).

The first explorer to travel by land into the area now known as Queensland was John Oxley who, in 1823, discovered the Tweed River and recommended Moreton Bay as a suitable location for a penal colony.

The establishment of a penal colony at Moreton Bay in 1824 prevented the further development of the area for nearly twenty years. The government decided to prevent any free settlers entering the area around the colony and this law remained until 1842 when Governor Gipps declared that 'all settlers and other free persons shall be at liberty to proceed to the Darling Downs in like manner as to any other part of the Colony.'

The settlement of Moreton Bay in 1824 led inevitably to a more serious assessment of the coast. Whaling boats and light craft sailed up the coast, the narrow strait between Fraser Island and the mainland was discovered, and the Mary and Burnett Rivers were explored.

The character of the area changed dramatically when Queensland (at the time it was still part of New South Wales) was opened up to free settlers. Almost immediately settlers moved into the coastal area and crops of sugar cane were grown while dairy and beef cattle were raised in the hinterland.

Brisbane from Bowen Terrace in the 1880s.

Pastoralists from the south moved large flocks of sheep north to take advantage of the good soils. The graziers, with their substantial production of wool, hides and tallow, forced the opening up of a number of ports on the coast. Suddenly the colony was booming.

Although the Darling Downs had been discovered and explored by Europeans as early as the 1820s (Allan Cunningham passed through the area in 1823) it wasn't until the government allowed squatters and pastoralists to move onto the rich and fertile plains that the area was settled.

Consequently many of the towns on the Darling Downs date their origins to the establishment of a specific land holding in the early 1840s. A town like Dalby, for example, dates its origins to a river crossing where a solitary white man lived and where the itinerant rural workers would pause for a rest and a drink as they passed through to the properties which lay to the west.

In 1844 Jimbour Station was the furthest outpost of European settlement. Beyond it lay an unexplored wilderness. It was the last European settlement visited by Ludwig Leichhardt before he made his epic 5000 kilometre trek from the Darling Downs across to Port Essington.

Leichhardt had been in Australia for two years when he heard of plans for an expedition from Sydney to Port Essington—an outpost on the coast of the Northern Territory. The expedition was to be led by Sir Thomas Mitchell but the Governor of the time, Governor Gipps, declared that it was 'an expedition of so hazardous and expensive a nature, without the knowledge and consent of the Colonial Office.' Irritated by this delay Leichhardt organised his own expedition. With a party of six he left Sydney on 13 August 1844. They were joined by another four people in Moreton Bay. They then rode to Jimbour and on 1 October headed west. For the next fifteen months they traversed western Queensland and the north-eastern section of the Northern Territory arriving at Port Essington, exhausted, on 17 December 1845. When they finally returned to Sydney on 25 March 1846 Leichhardt was greeted as a hero and hailed as the 'Prince of Explorers'.

As a result of Leichhardt's glowing reports on the land beyond Jimbour there was a push for settlement of the Dawson River area and the Central Western region of Queensland.

The settlers who followed Leichhardt's recommendations opened up the area to the north of the Darling Downs. This was a region of large land holdings which was hugely productive.

During the 1850s settlers pushed north into the Central Highlands where they met with strong resistance from the local Aborigines. The area around Taroom gained a reputation as one of the bloodiest killing fields in Australia. The local Aborigines, the Yeeman, fought for their land against the encroachment of European graziers. They fought with such determination that they were eventually wiped out. In the process a man named Billy Fraser almost certainly killed over one hundred members of the tribe making him the greatest mass murderer in Australian history.

Beyond the hills and valleys of the Great Dividing Range lay the vast, flat near-desert of the Gulf country and the Great Artesian Basin. This area was first explored by Burke and Wills who, in 1860, with a bizarre disregard for common

sense and the rules of exploration, led an expedition from Melbourne to the Gulf of Carpentaria. The Australian Dictionary of Biography entry on Robert O'Hara Burke makes the observations that 'it took four months to do the 1500 miles. They walked from 5 am to 5 pm with only a single day of rest in the whole period...It was magnificent, but it was not exploration. Burke kept no journal; there was no time for scientific observation, and nothing useful was discovered. Indirectly, discovery was promoted because, although Burke's own journey was worthless as exploration, solid gains in geographical knowledge were made by the explorers Howitt, McKinlay and Landsborough, who led parties in search of him'.

The expeditions of William Landsborough, Frederick Walker and John McKinlay scoured the area for the ill-fated Burke and Wills and in the process discovered both the pastoral and mining potential of the Gulf. William Landsborough referred, somewhat inaccurately, to the area as the 'Plains of Promise', John McKinlay noted the presence of copper near the present-day site of Cloncurry, and Frederick Walker sent back glowing reports of the region's pastoral potential.

Scenes near Bowen in the 1880s.

The first settler into the area was the remarkable Duncan McIntyre who followed Burke and Wills up the Darling River and settled in the area in 1865 at Dalgonally Station north of Julia Creek. He was followed in the 1870s and 1880s by settlers who carried out what could reasonably be described as a 'land grab'. Pastoralists moved in and claimed huge areas of the land which they stocked with cattle.

This pastoral industry was the basis of Queensland's economic success for nearly a century. Beef cattle and the wool industry began to decline in importance in the 1960s when synthetic fibres and the establishment of the European Economic Community played havoc with traditional markets.

The next major development occurred when gold was discovered in Gympie, along the Palmer River and at various points on the Atherton Tablelands. This was in the 1860s and 1870s and did much to open up the ports on the colony's northern coastline.

The towns which began to appear on the coast were all built for one reason: to provide port access. At first it was port access for the mineral wealth which was being dug out of the hinterland. Townsville, Cardwell, Port Douglas, Cairns and Cooktown all started life as ports from which gold could be shipped out. Later it became sugar with towns like Innisfail, Ingham and Mourilyan springing up. It was to these towns in the late nineteenth century that Polynesian labour, known as 'kanakas', was brought to harvest the sugar.

The construction of the ports was no great challenge. The real challenge was finding routes from the tablelands down the steep escarpment to the coast. Not only were the early trail blazers—men like Christie Palmerston, John Atherton and Bill Smith—confronted with sheer cliffs but they also had to deal with dense rainforest and local

Aborigines who were far from happy about the incursions made into their territory.

It was John Atherton, after whom the tablelands are named, who first brought cattle into the area. He realised that the miners needed to be fed and overlanded cattle to the Herberton fields. The result is that today the Atherton Tablelands are still a highly productive beef and dairy area.

Historically the coast was settled by farmers and fishermen. The ports grew to meet rural demands. Thus Cairns was originally created as a sugar and timber port. It became a meat exporting centre after World War II.

The result of this development is that Queensland's population distribution is dramatically different from that of other Australian states. Nearly half of the state's population lives in the greater Brisbane area. A further 34 per cent live in centres with populations of over 1000 people. In terms of its relatively small population Queensland has more cities over 20 000 than any other state, in fact eleven including Brisbane, Gold Coast, Sunshine Coast, Townsville, Toowoomba, Rockhampton, Cairns, Mackay, Bundaberg, Mt Isa and Gladstone.

By the turn of the century the coastal areas were becoming a tourist mecca for Queenslanders and visitors from the southern states.

The modern Gold Coast was really the inspiration of one man—Jim Cavill. In 1933 Elston was renamed Surfers Paradise and Cavell built his famous hotel which had a small zoo and a huge garden. It began to attract tourists.

During World War II the hotel was used by servicemen from all over the country who were so impressed by the area that they returned with their families in the early 1950s.

As beef and wool declined in importance the tourist potential of the coast grew. The coast had always attracted the adventurous traveller. In the 1940s big game fishermen from all over the world travelled to Cairns to try and catch marlin. The American western writer, Zane Gray, made a series of short movies of his fishing exploits off the coast of Cairns.

In the 1960s the area around Coolangatta began to grow and by the 1970s it was recognised as the premier beach resort on the east coast.

Modern-day Queensland has, at its heart, a great contradiction. Until thirty years ago it relied on beef, dairy products, wool and sugar cane for its wealth. It now relies on minerals and tourism, and preferably international tourism. The idea of farmers trying to develop one of the world's most beautiful coastlines and trying to match wits with aggressive developers is absurd. Yet it is precisely this absurdity which is the cornerstone of modern-day Queensland.

Recently there has been a continuing argument about the utilisation of resources. In the case of the state's greatest treasure, the Great Barrier Reef, it is fair to say that since 1975, when the Federal Government enacted the Great Barrier Reef Marine Park Act, that it has been accepted that the reef must not be mined or damaged and that its primary function must remain as an area of low-level tourism and scientific investigation. In 1981 it was accepted for World Heritage listing.

For most of this century Queensland's political life has been remarkably stable. The Labor Party held office from 1915 to 1957 (except for the period from 1929 to 1932) and then the Liberal–Country (later the Liberal-National) Party held office until the Labor Party under Wayne Goss regained power. After a brief return to the Liberal-National Party, though with a greatly reduced majority, the state is now back in the hands of the Labor Party under the premiership of Peter Beatty. Today the state, although driven by its rural wealth, has a good future based on the desire of large numbers of people from New South Wales and Victoria to move north to retire—a situation which will continue until the next century. It also has a successful tourism industry with more than 60 per cent of people who visit Australia nominating Queensland as their prime destination.

ABOVE: The city of Brisbane, on the banks of the Brisbane River, is the third largest city in Australia and the busiest river port.

ABOVE: Brisbane's colourful night lights throw shimmering reflections onto the Brisbane River.

BELOW: This Arbor in Brisbane's Southbank complex which was built on the Expo '88 site.

BELOW: Luxury residences and pleasure craft at Sanctuary Cove, an exclusive complex on Hope Island.

The William Jolly Bridge (ABOVE) and the Story Bridge (BELOW) are two of several bridges spanning the Brisbane River to link the city with its spreading suburbs.

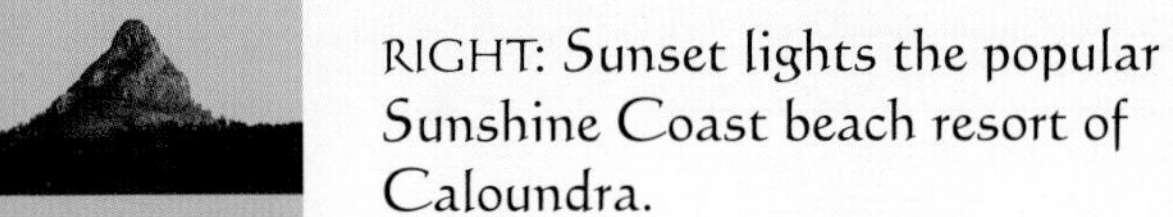

RIGHT: Sunset lights the popular Sunshine Coast beach resort of Caloundra.

BELOW: The Tropical Display Dome, one of the features of the Mt Coottha Botanic Gardens, Brisbane.

OPPOSITE, TOP: A Gold Coast landmark—Jupiters Casino at Broadbeach.

OPPOSITE, BOTTOM: Looking over an expanse of sand from the beach resort of Coolangatta to its sister city, Tweed Heads, across the border in New South Wales.

DOYLES

LEFT: Modern freeways skirt the Brisbane River in the city of Brisbane.

BELOW: Flower show in Laurel Bank Park in the garden city of Toowoomba. A Carnival of Flowers is held here every September.

OPPOSITE, TOP LEFT: Fishermen on the tranquil Maroochy River, Maroochydore, in the centre of the Sunshine Coast.

OPPOSITE, TOP RIGHT: Windsurfing off Caloundra, one of the many very popular beach resorts on the Sunshine Coast.

OPPOSITE, MIDDLE LEFT: A gardener's delight—the historic and colourful railway station at Spring Bluff, near Toowoomba.

OPPOSITE, MIDDLE RIGHT: Pineapples and tropical fruits are grown extensively on the coastal plains near Nambour, home of the Big Pineapple, a major tourist attraction.

OPPOSITE, BOTTOM LEFT: Farmland is interspersed with lush rainforest in Brisbane's mountainous hinterland near Mt Glorious.

OPPOSITE, BOTTOM RIGHT: Burning the cane—the thick foliage is burnt off to prepare the cane for harvesting. Sugar growing is a major industry in north Queensland.

RIGHT: Botanic gardens at the small town of Cooroy near Noosa Heads.

BELOW: Noosa—the most northerly of the sunshine coast resorts—has a unique combination of national park, beach, river and lake scenery.

ABOVE: The dunes of Cooloola National Park in a region noted for its high dune formations, wind driven sandblows and multi-coloured sand cliffs.

BELOW: Enjoying the rock pools at Jourama Falls in Jourama National Park, north-west of Townsville.

BELOW: A river of white-water rapids, huge jumbled boulders and tumbling falls churns its way through Mossman Gorge National Park near Daintree.

ABOVE: The rocky volcanic cores of the Glasshouse Mountains rise steeply out of the surrounding countryside. A rock climber's paradise, these mountains were named by Captain Cook in 1770.

BELOW, LEFT: One of more than one hundred koalas living at the Lone Pine Koala Sanctuary in Brisbane. Established in 1927 and occupying 20 hectares it is open daily and is also home to many other Australian native animals.

BELOW: The many hues of ochre, yellow, gold and brown in the coloured sands of Fraser Island, the world's largest sand island.

ABOVE: Four-wheel-drives and inflatable boats are both ideal modes of transport near Eli Creek on Fraser Island.

ABOVE: Airlie Beach, the main resort town on the Whitsunday Coast.

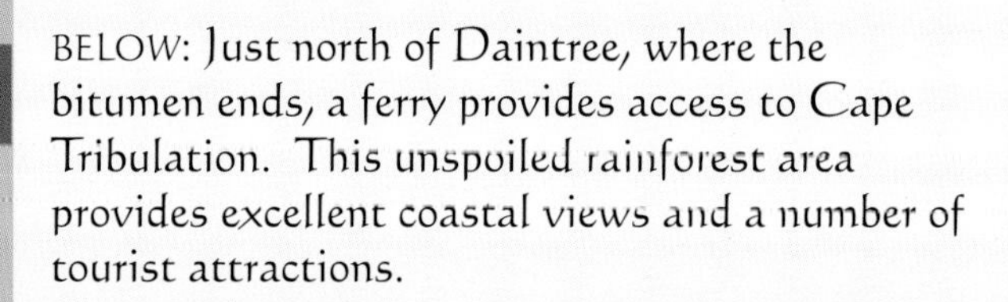

BELOW: Just north of Daintree, where the bitumen ends, a ferry provides access to Cape Tribulation. This unspoiled rainforest area provides excellent coastal views and a number of tourist attractions.

ABOVE: Elebana Falls, one of the many exquisite waterfalls in the Lamington National Park which can be found in the Gold Coast hinterland.

OPPOSITE: Shute Harbour—the ideal setting-off point to explore the many tropical islands in the beautiful Whitsunday waters.

BELOW: Harvest time at Australia's only commercial tea plantation at Nerada, west of Innisfail.

ABOVE: Windblown palms line the Johnstone River at Innisfail, south of Cairns.

OPPOSITE: Once a goldrush port, Port Douglas is now a popular resort offering tropical holidays on long beaches fringed with palms.

ABOVE: The Birdsville Hotel, about 100 years old, is the perfect overnight stop for tourists travelling down the infamous Birdsville track into South Australia.

OPPOSITE: Sunrise reflections on the Diamantina River, near Birdsville.

BELOW: Aboriginal rock paintings of sacred and ceremonial significance are a feature of the breathtakingly scenic Carnarvon National Park.

LEFT: A twentieth-century carving of Robert O'Hara Burke at Cooper Creek, just inside the Queensland border. This was the site of the last camp made by Burke and Wills on their tragic overland journey from Melbourne to the Gulf of Carpentaria.

BELOW: Pleasure craft moored at the peaceful seaside town of Port Douglas.

OPPOSITE: Lady Elliot Island at the southern tip of the Great Barrier Reef is a true reef island, a sand cay surrounded by coral reefs.

ABOVE: Tourists in four-wheel drive vehicles often cross the dry and harsh Simpson Desert.

OVERLEAF: Tangalooma, a pleasant tourist resort nestled in among the wilderness on Moreton Island, is a popular base for big-game fishing.

ABOVE: The water bore at Birdsville —the most isolated town in Queensland.

BELOW: The railway station at Normanton, the main town of the Gulf Country, is a monument to the goldrush days.

ABOVE: Aboriginal dancers at Laura on the Cape York Peninsula.

BELOW: Young locals line up to be photographed for posterity at Cunnamulla, a friendly sheep town on the Warrego River north of the New South Wales border.

OPPOSITE: Reputedly Australia's widest waterfall, Millstream Falls is situated in eucalypt woodlands on the eastern slopes of the Atherton Tableland.

ABOVE: Cool greens colour the Gregory River near Gregory Downs in the Gulf Country—a vast, remote region that has more rivers than roads.

OPPOSITE: Tropical vegetation and sheer red, orange and grey cliffs line the Lawn Hill Creek which snakes through the Constance Range on its way to the Gulf of Carpentaria.

ABOVE: Patterned sand dunes in the the Simpson Desert.

ABOVE: Wallaman Falls, where Storm Creek plunges 278 metres down sheer dark cliffs onto boulders and rainforest below. Situated in Wallaman Falls National Park, close to Ingham, these falls are the third longest in the world.

TOP: The fast-flowing Broken River passes through rugged mountain terrain and luxuriant rainforest in the Eungella National Park on the central coast.

ABOVE: Grassland and rainforest clothe the hilly resort island of South Molle in the middle of the Whitsunday Passage.

The March of Time: **1788 to 1800**

1788–89	1790–92	1793–94	1795–97	1798–1800

EVENTS

1788 In January the First Fleet arrives at Botany Bay and six days later moves to Port Jackson.

1789 The Hawkesbury River, the Nepean River and the Blue Mountains, NSW, are discovered by an expedition led by Watkin Tench.

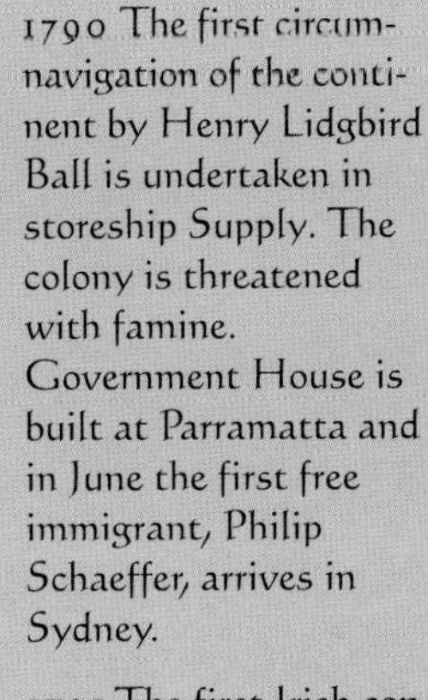

1790 The first circumnavigation of the continent by Henry Lidgbird Ball is undertaken in storeship Supply. The colony is threatened with famine. Government House is built at Parramatta and in June the first free immigrant, Philip Schaeffer, arrives in Sydney.

1791 The first Irish convicts arrive in Australia.

1792 The British government allows free settlers to take up land in NSW.

1793 Elizabeth Farm is built by John Macarthur. It is now the oldest extant building in Australia.

1794 The Reverend Samuel Marsden arrives in Sydney.

1795 George Bass and Matthew Flinders explore the Georges River and Botany Bay in the Tom Thumb.

1796 Port Hacking, Lake Illawarra and Port Kembla are discovered and explored by Bass and Flinders.

1797 Coal deposits are found south of Botany Bay and Captain John Shortland discovers coal in his exploration of the Hunter River area.

1798 Bass and Flinders begin journey to discover if Van Diemens Land is an island.

1799 Aborigines opposing the settlements at Parramatta and in the Hawkesbury River area suffer severe reprisals.

1800 A Customs House opens in Sydney and the first taxes are levied on beer, wine and spirit imports.

GOVERNMENT AND FOREIGN AFFAIRS

1788 In January Captain Arthur Phillip becomes the first Governor of the colony of NSW and in February the Colony of NSW is officially proclaimed by Judge Advocate David Collins.

1789 The colony establishes its first police force.

1790 A ticket-of-leave system is introduced by Governor Phillip.

1791 The Third Fleet arrives carrying 1763 convicts.

1792 In December Governor Phillip is forced to return to England because of ill health. Francis Grose becomes Acting Governor and replaces civil magistrates with military officers.

1793 The NSW Corps earns the name 'Rum Corps' by their illegal trading in liquor.

1794 Francis Grose is replaced by Captain William Paterson as administrator of the colony and head of the NSW Corps.

1795 John Hunter, who captained the Sirius in the First Fleet, becomes Governor of NSW.

1796 John Macarthur and the Rum Corps constantly oppose John Hunter.

1797 The first merino sheep are imported into the colony.

1798 Richard Dore succeeds David Collins as Deputy Judge-Advocate.

1799 Coal is exported to India from Newcastle.

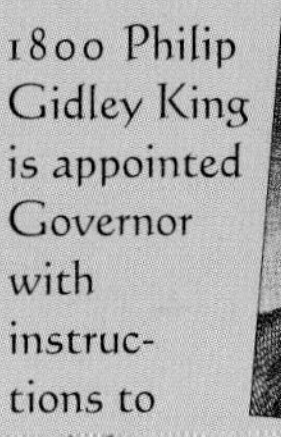

1800 Philip Gidley King is appointed Governor with instructions to end the monopoly of the Rum Corps.

LEISURE AND LIFESTYLE

1788 'The Rogue's March' becomes the first musical piece to be performed in public in the colony.

1789 A book entitled Narrative of the Expedition to Botany Bay by Watkin Tench is published in London.

1790 Journal of a Voyage to New South Wales by John White is published in London.

1791 James Ruse becomes the first self-sufficient farmer in the colony after receiving the first official land grant.

1792 The white population is estimated at 3120.

1793 The Reverend Richard Johnson establishes the first church in the colony in what is now Hunter Street, Sydney. It is destroyed by fire in 1798.

1793 John and Elizabeth Macarthur receive a land grant of 100 acres near Parramatta and establish a sheep-breeding farm.

1794 A settlement is established at Windsor.

1795 The first brewery in the colony is established by John Squires near Parramatta.

1796 The colony's first full-time playhouse and theatre opens in Bligh St, Sydney.

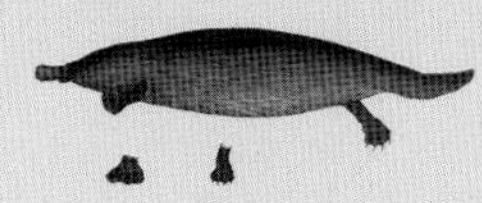

1797 First recorded sighting of the platypus by Europeans occurs.

1798 An Account of the English Colony in New South Wales by former Judge-Advocate David Collins is published in London.

1799 Whaling and sealing are becoming major industries.

1800 George Caley, naturalist and botanist, arrives to study Australian marsupials. John Lewin arrives and is the first professional artist and engraver.

The March of Time: 1801 to 1810

EVENTS

1801–02

1801 Matthew Flinders begins a two-year journey to circumnavigate and chart the entire continent.

1802 John Macarthur convinces the Privy Council in London to establish an Australian wool industry to overcome shortages in Europe. He is granted 10 000 acres and stock from King George III's flock.

1803–04

1803 Matthew Flinders returns from his complete circumnavigation of the continent.

1804 The first bale of colonial wool is sold in London by John Macarthur (above).

1805–06

1805 Macarthur chooses to take up his 10 000 acre land grant in the Cowpastures area and establishes his Camden Park Estate.

1806 Both flood and drought destroy crops and lead to a reduction in rations and increased costs.

1807–08

1807 The wool export trade begins with the shipment of a large consignment of wool to England.

1808 Governor Bligh is forcibly removed from office and imprisoned by Major Johnson and the NSW Corps in what was later known as the 'Rum Rebellion'.

1808 Stock and crops are damaged when the Hawkesbury River floods.

1809–10

1809 An official Post Office is established in Sydney.

1810 Governor Macquarie and his wife undertake a journey during which he plans and names the five 'Macquarie Towns': Richmond, Wilberforce, Pitt Town, Windsor and Castlereagh.

GOVERNMENT AND FOREIGN AFFAIRS

1801–02

1801 John Macarthur is sent to England for court-martial following a duel with Colonel Paterson, Commanding Officer of the NSW Corps.

1802 Lieutenant Charles Robbins is sent to Van Diemens Land to proclaim it a British possession when the French are suspected of planning to claim it for themselves.

1803–04

1803 The first settlement is established in Van Diemens Land, at Risdon Cove.

1804 An uprising by Irish convicts at Castle Hill is quickly put down by Major George Johnson and his Rum Corps but fifteen convicts are killed.

1805–06

1805 A merchant, Robert Campbell, attempts to break the trade monopoly of the East India Co. by exporting seal oil and skins directly to London instead of China.

1806 The new Governor, William Bligh (left), outlaws the use of rum for currency making enemies of the Rum Corps and John Macarthur.

1807–08

1807 John Macarthur and Captain Edward Abbott illegally import two rum stills. Governor Bligh prohibits their use.

1808 After the removal of Governor Bligh, Major Johnson administers the colony for seven months until Lieutenant-Colonel Joseph Foveaux arrives.

1809–10

1809 Lachlan Macquarie arrives to take up the post of Governor bringing with him a battalion of the 73rd Regiment to replace the recalled NSW Corps.

1810 Macquarie is sworn in on New Year's Day, promising justice for all.

LEISURE AND LIFESTYLE

1801–02

1801 Two Female Orphan Schools open.

1802 The first book is published in the colony, New South Wales General Standing Orders: Selected from the General Orders Issued by Former Governors.

1803–04

1803 The first suggestion of using the name 'Australia' (from Terra Australis, meaning 'Southland') is made by Matthew Flinders.

The first newspaper is published, the Sydney Gazette and New South Wales Advertiser, by George Howe.

1804 26 January is first celebrated as the colony's foundation day.

1805–06

1805 In August a cockfight near Sydney attracts large crowds of spectators and gamblers.

1806 The first triplets are born in the colony.

The term 'bushranger' is used for the first time, in the Sydney Gazette.

1807–08

1807 An emancipated surveyor, James Meehan, surveys and draws a map of Sydney Town.

A successful Scottish merchant Robert Campbell (above) begins building ships in Sydney.

1809–10

1809 The colony's first Presbyterian church is built at Ebenezer.

1810 The first government-approved horse race is held in Sydney. It is organised by the 73rd Regiment.

The March of Time: **1811 to 1820**

1811–12	1813–14	1815–16	1817–18	1819–20

EVENTS

1811 Macquarie visits Van Diemens Land and plans Hobart Town.

1812 For the first time a ship, the Indefatigable, brings convicts directly to Van Diemens Land from England.

1813 The Blue Mountains are finally crossed by Gregory Blaxland, William Wentworth and William Lawson.

1814 A road from Sydney to Liverpool via Parramatta opens and shortly after a coach service begins—the first public transport in the colony.

1815 William Cox and thirty convicts take just six months to complete a road across the Blue Mountains. Cox is rewarded with a land grant and the convicts with their freedom.

1816 The 'Rum Hospital' opens in Sydney.

1817 The Bank of NSW opens in Macquarie Place, Sydney. It is the first trading bank and public company in Australia.

1818 The Great Western Road linking Sydney and Parramatta to the Blue Mountains is opened, and the Hobart to Launceston road is finished.

1819 A new barracks for male convicts is opened at Hyde Park. The building still stands in Macquarie Street.

1820 St James Church of England in Sydney and Lancer Military Barracks in Parramatta, both designed by Francis Greenaway, are completed.

GOVERNMENT AND FOREIGN AFFAIRS

1811 In London, Macarthur is reprimanded and Johnson is cashiered for their actions during the 'Rum Rebellion'.

1812 Henry Bathurst is appointed Secretary of State for the Colonies and John Oxley (left) is appointed Surveyor-General of NSW.

1813 Currency shortages force Macquarie to use imported dollar coins as 'holey dollars' and 'dumps' (valued at five shillings and fifteen pence respectively), until 1824.

1814 The British government appoints Jeffrey Bent as the first judge of the Supreme Court of NSW.

1815 The white population is estimated at almost 15 000.

1816 A convict, Francis Greenaway, is appointed Civil Architect and Assistant Engineer by Macquarie, despite not having completed his fourteen-year sentence for forgery.

1817 John Macarthur returns to Sydney but is barred from public affairs.

1818 Justices of the Peace are empowered to hear complaints from employees as well as employers and to direct payment of wages.

1819 John Thomas Bigge is sent to Australia by the British Parliament to head a Commission of Inquiry into the state of affairs in NSW and Van Diemens Land.

1820 Sydney is visited by four Russian ships. The Russians set up a temporary observatory on Kirrabilli Point.

LEISURE AND LIFESTYLE

1811 A stone arch bridge over the Tank Stream connects east and west Sydney.

1812 The first recorded hunt using hounds is held by the newly established Sydney Hunt Club.

1813 Hoping to improve morality in the colony, Governor Macquarie decrees that part of each Sunday is to be devoted to religious duties.

1814 In a book published in London the day before his death, Matthew Flinders (below)

advocates the name Australia for the continent rather than New Holland.

1815 A school for Aboriginal children is established at Parramatta.

1816 The first Botanical Gardens are established in Sydney.

1817 Governor Macquarie uses the name 'Australia' in official correspondence to England.

1818 The first biography is published—a pamphlet by Thomas Wells based on the life of Michael Howe entitled The Last and Worst of the Bushrangers of Van Diemens Land.

1819 The 'Landholders, Merchants and other Respectable Inhabitants of the Colony' draw attention to social and economic grievances during a meeting in Sydney.

1820 The Roman Catholic church is established; the first Methodist service is held in Van Diemens Land; the first Jewish service is held and the first Australian Masonic Lodge is founded.

The March of Time: **1821 to 1830**

	1821–22	1823–24	1825–26	1827–28	1829–30
EVENTS	1821 The Port Macquarie penal settlement is opened. 1822 John Macarthur's wool sells for high prices in London and he is presented with two gold medals in recognition of its high quality. A penal settlement for difficult convicts is established at Macquarie Harbour, Van Diemens Land. 	1823 The first alluvial gold is discovered on the Fish River in NSW by James McBrien. 1824 Hamilton Hume and William Hovell set out on a journey of exploration to Spencer Gulf. 	1825 Richmond Bridge in Van Diemens Land is completed. It is now the oldest extant bridge in Australia. 1826 In an effort to forestall colonisation by the French, Governor Darling sends Major Edmund Lockyer to King George Sound to establish a settlement. It is the first settlement in Western Australia and the present site of Albany.	1827 Allan Cunningham leads an expedition to Moreton Bay. He discovers the Darling Downs and a gap through the Great Dividing Range which will provide access to the Darling Downs from Moreton Bay. 1828 An expedition led by Charles Sturt sets out to search for an inland sea by tracing the Macquarie River.	1829 Charles Sturt's expedition discovers the Darling River and explores the Bogan and Castlereagh rivers. 1830 A penal settlement, a place of severe punishment for repeat offenders, is established at Port Arthur, south-east of Hobart.
GOVERNMENT AND FOREIGN AFFAIRS	1821 Macquarie resigns and Major General Sir Thomas Makdougall Brisbane (above) becomes Governor. 1822 John Thomas Bigge's report is completed and published in London.	1823 An Act of Parliament is passed in London making NSW and Van Diemens Land separate colonies with each having an appointed Legislative Council. 1824 Governor Brisbane is forced to place the area around Bathurst under martial law after serious conflicts between whites and Aborigines.	1825 Ralph Darling becomes Governor. 1826 Governor Darling decides to make an example of two disgraced soldiers which leads to the Sudds and Thompson Case. Darling's bungling of the affair eventually leads to his departure from the colony.	1827 Governor Darling is prevented by the Chief Justice from passing a law to stifle press criticism of his administration. 1828 Sir Thomas Mitchell is appointed Surveyor-General, a position he holds for twenty-seven years.	1829 Governor James Stirling formally makes the entire continent of New Holland British Territory when he proclaims the settlement of Western Australia. 1830 Lieutenant-Governor George Arthur makes a disastrous attempt to round up all the remaining Aborigines in Van Diemens Land and force them to resettle on Flinders Island. However, his infamous 'Black Line' catches only one woman and a young boy.
LEISURE AND LIFESTYLE	1821 Michael Howe, The Terror of Van Diemen's Land by J. Amherst becomes the first Australian play to be performed on the London stage. 1822 Thirty-four bushrangers are sentenced to hang in Sydney as bushranging becomes a serious problem.	1823 Dr William Sherwin becomes the first Australian member of the Royal College of Physicians in London and Dr Henry Cowper, who first uses quinine to treat fever in Queensland, becomes the first Australian-born member of the Royal College of Surgeons. 1824 William Charles Wentworth and Robert Wardell begin the Australian, Australia's first privately-owned daily newspaper, just one day before the rigid censorship of the press is abolished.	 1825 Augustus Earle, portrait painter and topographical artist, arrives in Australia. 1826 The first oil lamp in an Australian street is lit in Macquarie Place, Sydney, and a Sydney shop records the first use of gaslight.	1827 The Colonial Museum (later the Australian Museum) is founded in Sydney. 1828 George Wyndham plants a vineyard on his property, Dalwood, in the Hunter Valley, which still produces wine today.	1829 One of the first notable industrial actions occurs in Australia when newspaper compositors in Sydney strike over wage reductions. 1830 Ex-convict John Savery's novel, Quintus Serviton, beomes the first novel to be written, printed and published in Australia.

The March of Time: **1831 to 1840**

1831–32	1833–34	1835–36	1837–38	1839–40

EVENTS

1831 The steamer Sophia Jane arrives from England to begin a regular service between Sydney and Parramatta.

1832 A road down the Victoria Pass in the Blue Mountains of NSW is completed under the supervision of Sir Thomas Mitchell, who then goes on to supervise the Sydney–Goulburn road.

1833 Australia's main exports are whale and seal products but as wool sales increase it begins to replace these as the country's primary industry.

1834 The first (unauthorised) settlement is established at Portland, Victoria, by Edward Henty.

1835 John Batman, after exploring the area around Geelong, makes a treaty with local Aborigines to 'purchase' 600 000 acres of land. The treaty is later disallowed by Governor Bourke.

1836 Major Thomas Mitchell's expedition explores the Murrumbidgee, Lachlan, Murray and Lodden rivers discovering rich grazing land. He refers to the land as 'Australia Felix'.

1837 Elizabeth Bay House in Sydney is completed and construction begins on St Andrews Cathedral..

1838 A settlement is established at Port Essington to provide a northern trading station.

1839 Angus McMillan enters East Gippsland and opens up land for agricultural purposes. Exploration of the Australian Alps is begun by Paul Edmund de Strzelecki, a Polish explorer and scientist.

1840 Paul Strzelecki climbs and names Australia's highest mountain, Mt Kosciuszko.

GOVERNMENT AND FOREIGN AFFAIRS

1831 The practice of giving free land grants to settlers is abolished and a system of land auctions is introduced.

1832 Assisted immigration begins when a shipload of female immigrants leaves England, their fares having been subsidised by the government.

1833 The House of Commons in London is petitioned for a more representative government following a large public meeting in Sydney.

1834 The South Australian Act is passed in British Parliament to establish a new, non-convict, 'planned' settlement in South Australia.

1835 The last of the Aborigines from Van Diemens Land is captured and sent to Flinders Island. George Robinson is appointed Protector of the 300 surviving Aborigines now living on the island.

1836 The Surveyor-General of South Australia, Colonel William Light, chooses an inland site for the settlement against recommendations for a coastal port site.

1837 The total white population is estimated to be 132 819.

1838 Twenty-eight Aboriginal men, women and children are massacred at Myall Creek. Seven white men are later hanged for the crime.

1839 The British government claims New Zealand and it becomes part of New South Wales. A year later it becomes a separate colony.

1840 Transportation of convicts from England to NSW ceases but will continue to Van Diemens Land and Norfolk Island.

LEISURE AND LIFESTYLE

1831 A four-page newspaper, the Sydney Herald, begins production in April. In 1842 it was renamed the Sydney Morning Herald and is now the oldest extant newspaper in the Southern Hemisphere.

1832 Two Anglican Kings Schools open, one in Sydney and one at Parramatta (above), to bring higher education to the sons of wealthy colonists.

1833 The first School of Arts and Mechanics Institute is founded in Sydney.

1834 A NSW Temperance Society is formed in Sydney.

1835 The 'Wild White Man', William Buckley, an escaped convict, surrenders after living with Aborigines for thirty-two years in the Port Phillip Bay area. He is granted a free pardon.

1836 The naturalist Charles Darwin visits Sydney on HMS Beagle (left).
William Grant Broughton (right) is consecrated Bishop of Australia.

1837 The first Chinese agricultural-labourers arrive in Australia.

1838 Henry Parkes and his family arrive in Sydney in February as assisted immigrants and in September Caroline Chisholm arrives and begins her philanthropic work with young women.

1839 Opuntia stricta (prickly pear) is introduced into Australia from the Gulf of Mexico to the deep regret of later generations. It will be over 100 years before this pest is finally eradicated by the cactoblastis moth.

1840 Horseracing begins at the Flemington racecourse in Melbourne.

The March of Time: **1841 to 1850**

1841–42 | 1843–44 | 1845–46 | 1847–48 | 1849–50

EVENTS

1841 John Eyre becomes the first European to cross from Adelaide to Albany over land. The trip is hampered by lack of water, and two Aboriginal members of the party kill Eyre's assistant and steal all the food.

1842 Substantial deposits of copper are discovered in South Australia.

1843 Benjamin Boyd establishes a large whaling station at Twofold Bay in southern NSW.

1844 German naturalist, Ludwig Leichhardt, leads an expedition from the Darling Downs (Queensland) to Port Essington (Northern Territory). The journey takes fourteen months and covers 4800 kilometres.

1845 Government House in Sydney is completed.

The near extinction of whales causes a decline in the whaling industry.

1846 First proposals for a railway system are made at a public meeting led by James Macarthur, and the Sydney Tramroad and Railway Co. is established.

1847 Melbourne is declared a city.

1848 Ludwig Leichhardt's party disappears while trying to cross the continent from east to west.

1849 Young Thomas Chapman discovers gold north-west of Melbourne.

A uniform two-penny postage rate is introduced by the government.

1850 Western Australia's first convicts arrive at Swan River on board the Scindian.

GOVERNMENT AND FOREIGN AFFAIRS

1841 With very little help from the government, Caroline Chisholm establishes a Female Immigrants Home to shelter newly arrived females and to help them find work.

1842 In July, Sydney is incorporated as a city and, in August, Melbourne is incorporated as a town.

1843 A financial crisis in NSW is caused by drought, lack of wool sales, high bank interest rates and low wheat prices.

1844 The Pastoral Association is formed by squatters to fight new squatting regulations introduced by the NSW government.

1845 British troops are sent from Australia to New Zealand to fight in the Maori rebellion.

1846 Transportation of convicts to Van Diemens Land is halted for two years. Sir Charles Fitzroy is appointed governor.

1847 The forty-seven surviving Tasmanian Aborigines left on Flinders Island are returned to Van Diemens Land.

1848 Western Australia conducts its first official census, counting 11 976 people. Aborigines are not included.

1849 The wool industry grows rapidly, providing half of Britain's wool imports.

1850 The Australian League is formed by the Reverend John Dunmore Lang to promote a national republic, universal male suffrage and an end to convict transportation.

LEISURE AND LIFESTYLE

1841 The first volume of The Birds of Australia by John Gould is published in London.

1842 A North Shore ferry service begins in Sydney.

1843 John Bede Polding (right) arrives back in Sydney with nineteen Roman Catholic priests, brothers and students. The enthusiastic welcome they receive causes consternation among Sydney Protestants.

1844 The Currency Lass, a musical comedy by Edward Geoghegan, is first performed in Sydney.

1845 A crowd of about 10 000 gathers outside Darlinghurst Goal when murderer John Knatchbull is executed.

1846 The Moreton Bay Courier and the Melbourne Argus begin publication.

1847 The Hon. James Graham lays out a golf course on the site later known as Flagstaff Gardens, in Melbourne.

1848 John Gould completes his seven-volume work The Birds of Australia.

1849 Caroline Chisholm establishes the Family Colonization Loan Society in London to help prospective emigrants to Australia.

1850 Sir Thomas Mitchell and Stuart Donaldson exchange shots in a duel.

The March of Time: **1851 to 1860**

1851–52	1853–54	1855–56	1857–58	1859–60

EVENTS

1851 The goldrush begins, first in the area near Bathurst, then near Ballarat and Bendigo. Miners' licences are introduced.

1852 The township of Gundagai is flooded by the Murrumbidgee River, and more than eighty people drown.

1853 Paddlesteamers are first used on the Murray–Darling river system.

1854 S. W. McGowan completes the telegraph line between Melbourne and Williamstown, the first in Australia.

1855 A. C. Gregory leads an expedition south-east from the Victoria River and searches for traces of Leichhardt's party.

The first government-run steam railway in the British Empire is opened between Sydney and Parramatta.

1856 South Australia is granted responsible government.

1857 Two major shipwrecks occur off Sydney: the clippers Dunbar (121 lives lost) and Catherine Adamson (21 lives lost).

1858 John McDouall Stuart finds good sheep-grazing country in his exploration of South Australia.

1859 The building of Leonard Terry's design for the Melbourne Club is completed.

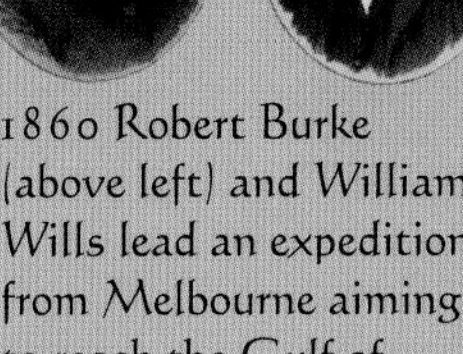

1860 Robert Burke (above left) and William Wills lead an expedition from Melbourne aiming to reach the Gulf of Carpentaria.

GOVERNMENT AND FOREIGN AFFAIRS

1851 The Port Phillip District becomes a separate colony named Victoria.

1852 The British government agrees to stop sending convicts to the eastern colonies.

1853 Gold becomes the country's chief export.

1854 Troops attack the Eureka Stockade, built by Ballarat goldminers to protest high mining licence fees and other injustices. Peter Lalor leads the miners.

1855 NSW, Victoria and Van Diemens Land are granted responsible government. Sir Charles Hotham becomes first Governor of Victoria.

1856 The name Van Diemens Land is officially changed to Tasmania.

1857 Anti-Chinese feelings intensify on the goldfields, and discriminatory laws are introduced.

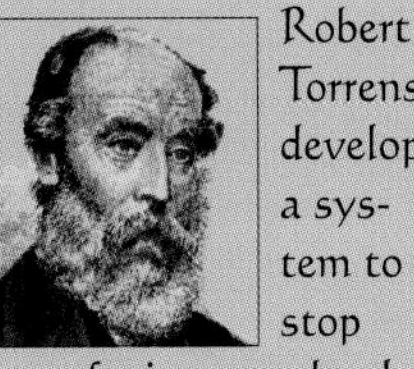

Robert Torrens develops a system to stop confusion over land titles when deeds are lost and land changes hands.

1858 Australia's white population reaches the one million mark.

1859 The new separate colony of Queensland is established and granted responsible government.

1860 The colonial warship, HMCS Victoria, is sent to New Zealand with British troops to help settlers fight Maoris.

LEISURE AND LIFESTYLE

1851 Two American Mormon missionaries arrive in Sydney. Scotch College is founded as the Melbourne Academy and the first Catholic and Presbyterian schools open in Melbourne.

1852 In South Australia, the government stops aid to denominational schools. The opera Norma is performed in Melbourne.

1853 The first Australian public library using government funds is opened in Melbourne, and the Victorian Fine Arts Society is founded.

1854 George Watson sets up the Melbourne Hunt Club. Opera singer Catherine Hayes visits Australia.

1855 The NSW government imposes a tariff on sugar, coffee, tea, tobacco and alcohol. The first recorded eisteddfod is held in Ballarat, Victoria.

1856 Stonemasons in NSW and building trades workers in Victoria win an eight-hour working day.

1857 The streets of Hobart and Melbourne are lit by gas. A pottery works is opened at Bendigo in Victoria. Fort Denison in Sydney Harbour is completed.

1858 The country's first Divorce Act is passed. Australian Rules football begins in Melbourne and the Melbourne Australian Rules Football Club is founded.

1859 Rabbits are introduced into Victoria as game animals.

1860 The Sydney Mail, published by John Fairfax (above) & Sons, begins publication.

The March of Time: **1861 to 1870**

1861–62	1863–64	1865–66	1867–68	1869–70

EVENTS

1861 Alfred Howitt's search party finds the only survivor of the Burke and Wills expedition.

1862 Cobb & Co.'s coach service, now owned by James Rutherford, extends its business into NSW.

1863 Work begins on the Adelaide Town Hall, designed by Edmund William Wright.

1864 Brisbane's city centre is ravaged by fires in April and December.

1865 Bushrangers Dan Morgan, Ben Hall (left) and John Gilbert are killed by gunshot in separate arrests.

1866 John McKinlay explores the country's north, looking for a coastal settlement site.

1867 A telegraph line links Sydney and Melbourne.

1868 An attempt is made on the life of visiting Prince Alfred, Duke of Edinburgh. The would-be assassin is hanged.

1869 The Zig-Zag Railway is completed, an important stage in the crossing of the Blue Mountains by rail.

1870 Construction begins of the 3000 kilometre long Overland Telegraph Line between Adelaide and Palmerston (later Darwin). It is completed in 1872.

GOVERNMENT AND FOREIGN AFFAIRS

1861 Violent anti-Chinese riots occur on the goldfields near Lambing Flat.

1862 A minimum age of thirteen is set for NSW coal miners working underground.

1863 Natives from the islands to the north-east of Australia are brought in to labour on Queensland cotton and sugar plantations.

1864 Commercial grade sugar is made from Queensland sugar cane at Louis Hope's new sugar mill.

1865 Coal is exported to Japan for the first time.

1866 Victoria introduces a protectionist tariff, a first for Australian colonies.

1867 NSW's anti-Chinese legislation is repealed.

1868 The transportation of convicts to Australia ends with the arrival of the last convict ship, the Hougomont, in Western Australia.

1869 George Goyder surveys the area around Port Darwin for a capital city for the Northern Territory. He names the site Palmerston.

1870 The colonies become responsible for their own defence with the departure of the remaining British forces.

LEISURE AND LIFESTYLE

1861 The Victorian Turf Club runs a new event, the Melbourne Cup, with the prize money of 200 sovereigns won by Archer, ridden by J. Cutts.

1862 (Right) Henry Kendall's Poems and Songs, his first work, is published.

1863 Western Australia passes divorce legislation.

1864 The Australasian (later the Australasian Post) begins publication.

1865 Brothers William and David Arnott set up a bakery business in Newcastle.

1866 Mother Mary McKillop establishes the sisters of St Joseph of the Sacred Heart as a teaching order of nuns.

1867 (Left) Adam Lindsay Gordon's first two poetry books are published.

1868 A cricket team of thirteen Aborigines has a successful season touring England, with 'Twopenny' the bowler the star attraction.

1869 The Agricultural Society of NSW has its first Exhibition (or 'Show'), at Belmore Park.

A nine-hole golf course is constructed in Adelaide.

1870 Eugene von Guèrard is appointed as head of the new Victorian Academy of Arts.

One day after the publication of his Bush Ballads and Galloping Rhymes Adam Lindsay Gordon commits suicide.

The March of Time: **1871 to 1880**

1871–72	1873–74	1875–76	1877–78	1879–80

EVENTS

1871 Alexander Forrest leads an exploratory expedition in Western Australia, successfully locating good farming land.

1872 The discovery of gold at Charters Towers, Queensland, prompts a goldrush there.

1873 Surveyor William Gosse discovers Ayers Rock, naming it after Sir Henry Ayers, Premier of South Australia. In the late twentieth century it is renamed Uluru.

1874 The estimated NSW Aboriginal population is 9000.

1875 Queensland, NSW, South Australia and Tasmania are all affected by floods.

1876 Australia and New Zealand are linked by an undersea telegraph cable from Sydney to Wellington.

1877 Severe drought affects all the colonies with huge losses of crops and animals.

1878 Telephones are established in Melbourne, the first one linking a hardware store with its head office.

The world's longest stock route, from Aramac in Queensland to the Daly River in the Northern Territory is explored and opened up by Nathaniel Buchanan.

1879 Alexander Forrest's expedition discovers good farming land around the Ord River in Western Australia.

1880 Two famous bushrangers are hanged: Captain Moonlight in NSW and Ned Kelly (above) in Victoria.

GOVERNMENT AND FOREIGN AFFAIRS

1871 The Queensland government attempts to supervise the recruitment of Pacific Islanders by plantation owners.

1872 Henry Parkes (right) begins his first term as Premier of NSW.

1873 Captain John Moresby claims New Guinea for Britain, but the British government repudiates his claim.

1874 NSW exports wool to Japan for the first time.

1875 The Derwent ironworks in Tasmania and the Eskbank ironworks at Lithgow begin smelting operations.

1876 Males aged 13–18 are limited to a 50½ hour working week by the NSW Coal Mines Act.

1877 The Port Arthur penal station (left) is closed down.

1878 The Victorian government is in chaos as Premier Berry tries to force the legislative council to pass a supply bill.

1879 The NSW government dedicates about 8000 hectares of land for use as a 'national park'. The Sutherland National Park is the country's first.

1880 Peter Lalor (left) previously arrested for his part in the Eureka Stockade, becomes speaker of the Victorian Legislative Assembly.

LEISURE AND LIFESTYLE

1871 The Ballarat School of Mines is opened, giving Victoria its first technical college.

Australia's first sheepdog trials are held at Forbes in NSW. The winner, a bitch named Kelpie, gives the breed its name.

1872 Frederick Wolseley builds a working model of a sheep shearing machine.

1873 Edward William Cole (above) opens his Book Arcade in Bourke Street, Melbourne.

1874 Smallpox vaccinations are made compulsory for Victorian infants.

1875 T. S. Mort's (above) refrigeration company brings chilled milk to Sydney from dairy farms in the country.

1876 Edward Trickett wins the first world sculling championship, becoming Australia's first world sporting champion.

1877 The Sydney Morning Herald begins publishing a weather map, with a weather forecast for the day.

1878 The first artesian bore brings water to the surface near Bourke, NSW.

1879 An American actor, J. C. Williamson, stages Gilbert and Sullivan's H.M.S. Pinafore, the first of his many productions.

1880 Journalists John Haynes and John Archibald (left) begin publication of the Bulletin newspaper.

The March of Time: **1881 to 1890**

1881–82	1883–84	1885–86	1887–88	1889–90

EVENTS

1881 A smallpox epidemic begins in Sydney eventually claiming about forty lives.

1882 Firemen are powerless as Sydney's 'Garden Palace' is destroyed by fire. The Palace was built for the International Exhibition of 1880.

1883 The NSW and Victorian railway lines are linked, with passengers travelling from Sydney to Melbourne only needing to change trains at Albury.

1884 The master and crew of the Hopeful are found guilty of the murder of Pacific Islanders they had 'recruited' for work on Queensland sugar plantations.

1885 Western Australia's first goldrush begins near Halls Creek after finds made by Charles Hall and Jack Slattery.

1886 Californian irrigation experts George and William Chaffey sign an agreement with the Victorian government to pioneer irrigated farming on the Murray River at Mildura.

1887 The practice of naming cyclones is introduced to arouse public interest in the weather bureau.

1888 Tamworth in NSW becomes the first country town in Australia to introduce electric street lighting.

1889 Lawrence Hargrave invents the rotary engine and develops a model of a flying machine powered by compressed air.

1890 Dr Emma Constance Stone becomes the first registered woman doctor in Australia.

GOVERNMENT AND FOREIGN AFFAIRS

1881 Australia's first simultaneous census is taken. It reveals that the white population has reached two million.

1882 The British government gives the screw corvette, Wolverine, to NSW, to be used as a training ship.

1883 The Intercolonial Conference, attended by the colonies' leaders, agree to form a Federal Australasian Council to legislate on matters affecting the whole country.

1884 The governments of NSW, South Australia, and Queensland introduce relief work to deal with high unemployment.

1885 Troops from NSW leave to join the British troops in the Sudan after the death of General Gordon at Khartoum.

1886 The Victorian Wharf Labourers' Union strikes for the eight-hour day, the first strike to be settled by arbitration.

1887 Rallies protesting against Chinese immigration are held in Sydney.

1888 The British New Guinea (Papua) Protectorate becomes a Crown Colony administered by Queensland and Great Britain.

1889 Lack of hygienic sewage disposal in Melbourne results in 558 deaths from typhoid. Victoria establishes a Department of Public Health.

1890 The maritime strike over the right to unionism spreads to other industries in eastern and southern Australia causing industrial chaos. This strike is the first major clash between employers and the trade union movement in Australia.

LEISURE AND LIFESTYLE

1881 The Art Gallery of South Australia is opened.

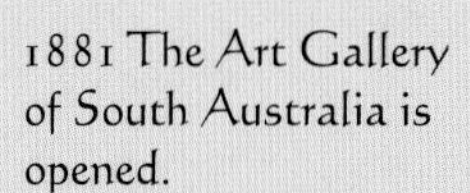

1882 The Sydney Mail begins publishing Rolf Boldrewood's (above) Robbery Under Arms in serial form.

1883 The Servants Training Institution is opened in Melbourne to train young women for domestic service.

1884 Hugh McKay demonstrates his stripper harvester, an invention to make wheat harvesting easier.

Bare knuckled boxing is declared illegal after the death of a boxer at Randwick, NSW.

1885 A party of Seventh Day Adventist ministers and their families arrive in Melbourne.

The National Gallery of NSW opens in Sydney.

1886 The remodelled Princess Theatre opens in Melbourne with a performance of Gilbert and Sullivan's The Mikado.

The first Angus & Robertson bookshop opens in Sydney.

1887 Henry Lawson, (left) aged twenty, has his first poem, 'Song of the Republic', published in the Bulletin.

1888 J. T. Williams gives the first demonstration in Australia of a parachute when he jumps out of a balloon over Sydney.

1889 The Heidelberg School of artists opens its first large exhibition of impressionist art in Melbourne. It is condemned by leading art critics.

1890 'Banjo' Paterson's bush ballad, 'The Man From Snowy River', is first published in the Bulletin.

The March of Time: **1891 to 1900**

1891–92	1893–94	1895–96	1897–98	1899–1900

EVENTS

1891 H. Jones and Co. of Hobart (IXL label) pioneers fruit canning in Australia.

1892 The complete skeleton of the prehistoric marsupial, Diprotodon, which grew to the size of a large rhinoceros, is found at Lake Callabonna, South Australia.

1893 Patrick Hannan and friends discover gold nuggets at Kalgoorlie, Western Australia, an area which becomes known as the Golden Mile.

1894 Frances Knorr is found guilty of murdering babies and hanged in Melbourne. Mrs Knorr ran a business where unmarried mothers paid her to act as a foster parent to their unwanted babies.

1895 Very low rainfall this year begins a pattern which continues until 1902 causing a seven-year national drought. It hampers recovery from an economic depression which reduced sheep numbers by 50% and cattle by 40%.

1896 Sir William Henry Bragg pioneers the use of the X-ray in Australia.

1897 The NSW Post Office first officially uses bicycles to deliver the mail.

1898 William Farrar (above) produces two successful strains of drought resistant wheat.

1899 John Norton, editor of the Sydney Truth, coins the word 'wowser' to describe puritanical fanatics.

1900 Aborigines Jimmy and Joe Governor and Jackie Underwood kill nine people in NSW during the year. Joe Governor is shot and Jimmy and Underwood are hanged.

GOVERNMENT AND FOREIGN AFFAIRS

1891 Three Labour candidates win seats in the South Australian elections, the first Labour Party members elected to an Australian parliament.

1892 Queensland becomes the first government to introduce the 'preferential' voting system which was later adopted by the Federal Parliament in 1918.

1893 Banks close due to a financial crisis. Thousands of small investors are very distressed.

1894 The South Australian government gives women the right to vote and to stand for both houses of parliament—the first Australian colony to do so.

1895 The Closer Settlement Act is passed in NSW making land available to farmers on easy terms on the condition it is lived on and improved.

1896 Women vote for the first time in Australia at an election for the House of Assembly in South Australia.

1897 Queensland adopts the Aboriginal Protection Act which transfers the control of Aboriginal reserves from missions to the government.

1898 The NSW government creates a Bureau of Statistics and publishes the first statistics on childbirth and infant mortality.

1899 The first contingent of Australian troops leaves for South Africa to support Britain in the Boer War.

1900 Edmund Barton (above) becomes Australia's first Prime Minister.

LEISURE AND LIFESTYLE

1891 The famous French actress, Sarah Bernhardt, makes her first Australian appearance at Her Majesty's Theatre, Sydney.

1892 The first Sheffield Shield cricket match played between NSW, Victoria and South Australia is won by Victoria.

1893 The Tivoli Variety circuit begins and the first classical ballet choreographed in Australia is performed at the Princess Theatre, Melbourne.

1894 Ethel Turner publishes her first novel, Seven Little Australians.

1895 'Banjo' Patterson composes the lyrics for the folk song, 'Waltzing Matilda'. It is first sung in public at the North Gregory Hotel in Winton, central Queensland.

1896 Edwin Flack, a Victorian and the only Australian competitor, wins the men's 800 metres and 1500 metres foot races at the first modern Olympic Games held in Athens.

1897 Walter Withers is the first to win the Wynne Art Prize for his painting, The Storm.

Artist Datillo Rubbo opens an art school in Sydney.

1898 In Sydney, Greeks and Lebanese build a Christian Orthodox Church, the first in Australia.

The Christian Science Church holds its first services in Australia, in Melbourne.

1899 Major Joseph Perry of the Salvation Army begins work on Soldiers of the Cross, the first commercial film made in Australia.

1900 Frederick Lane wins Australia's first gold medal for swimming at the Olympic Games in Paris.

The March of Time: **1901 to 1910**

1901–02	1903–04	1905–06	1907–08	1909–10

EVENTS

1901 The Australian flag is flown for the first time.

1902 The Pacific Cable linking Southport, Queensland, with Vancouver, Canada, by submarine telegraph cable is opened, thus establishing trans-Pacific cable communications.

1903 The following newspapers are first published this year: the Brisbane Daily Mail, the Sunday Sun (Sydney), the Border Morning Mail (Albury), and the People's Daily (Melbourne).

1904 Electricity cables are laid across Sydney Harbour (right) to provide household power and electric street lighting.

1905 The Header Harvester is invented by Massey-Harris Co. It enables the harvesting of rain-damaged wheat crops.

1906 The Marconi Co. officially establishes wireless telegraphy between Queenscliff, Victoria, and Devonport, Tasmania.

1907 In Western Australia, the 'No. 1 Rabbit Proof Fence' is completed after five years work but is unsuccessful in stopping the spread of rabbits into that state.

1908 The 'great white fleet' of the US Navy begins a month-long visit to Australia.

1909 Severe flooding occurs in north-western NSW, south-eastern Queensland and the south-west of South Australia.

1910 W. E. Raymond, the NSW Government Astronomer, photographs Halley's Comet on its transit of the sun.

GOVERNMENT AND FOREIGN AFFAIRS

1901 The Commonwealth of Australia comes into being at an inaugural ceremony in Centennial Park, Sydney, on the first day of the 20th century.

1902 Women are granted the right to vote in federal elections.

1903 The Commonwealth Defence Act is passed making military service compulsory in time of war.

1904 The recruitment of kanakas to work in the Queensland cane-fields ceases.

1905 Western Australia, following Queensland's example, passes an Aboriginal Protection Act which establishes reserves and 'protectors', tightening control over many aspects of Aboriginal life.

1906 The colony of British New Guinea is re-named Papua and comes under Australian administrative control.

1907 The concept of a basic or minimum wage is legally established by Mr Justice Higgins when he hands down the Harvester Judgement. Initially it was seven shillings per day for a six-day working week.

1908 The Commonwealth government passes a bill for old-age and invalid pensions of ten shillings per week.

1909 The Federal Defence Act is introduced and provides for the establishment of a military college and compulsory military training for males aged 12–26.

1910 The first Australian coins and banknotes are issued.

LEISURE AND LIFESTYLE

1901 My Brilliant Career by Miles Franklin is published.

1902 The soprano, Nellie Melba, gives her first recital in Brisbane after returning from Europe.

1903 Such is Life by Joseph Furphy is published.

1904 W. A. Barton is selected as Australia's first Rhodes Scholar.

1905 The first Melbourne–Sydney motor racing reliability trial is held. Mrs Ben Thompson is the first woman competitor.

1906 The Story of the Kelly Gang, thought to be one of the first feature-length films in the world, is screened in Melbourne.

1907 Australia wins the Davis Cup for the first time.

1908 Australia's first surf carnival is held at Manly. The Bondi club demonstrates the march past drill.

1909 Singers Peter Dawson and Amy Castles tour Australia and Dame Nellie Melba makes her third concert tour.

1910 Cozens Spencer's narrative film, The Life and Adventures of John Vane, the Notorious Australian Bushranger, premieres in Melbourne.

The March of Time: **1911 to 1920**

1911–12	1913–14	1915–16	1917–18	1919–20

EVENTS

1911 J. J. Hammond makes the first significant powered aircraft flight in Australia carrying passengers.

1912 The Commonwealth Bank, owned and operated by the Federal government, opens as a savings bank.

1913 The first penny postage stamp of the Commonwealth of Australia is issued. It is known as the kangaroo series, or 'roo' stamp.

1914 Australia's first official airmail delivery is made from Melbourne to Sydney—1785 letters are delivered.

1915 BHP opens its steelworks at Newcastle and begins large-scale steel production.

1916 The Taronga Zoological Park opens in Sydney.

1917 Due to anti-German feelings in South Australia, the names of over forty towns and districts with German origins are changed. German-speaking schools and newspapers are also closed down.

1918 (Left) Sydney receives the first direct overseas radio telephone transmission message sent in morse code from Britain.

1919 A worldwide influenza epidemic kills 11 552 Australians.

1920 Queensland and Northern Territory Aerial Services Ltd, now known as Qantas, is founded.

GOVERNMENT AND FOREIGN AFFAIRS

1911 The newly formed Naval Board officiallly promulgates an order which establishes the Royal Australian Navy in October.

1912 A maternity allowance of five pounds per child, known as the 'Baby Bonus', is paid to all white Australian mothers.

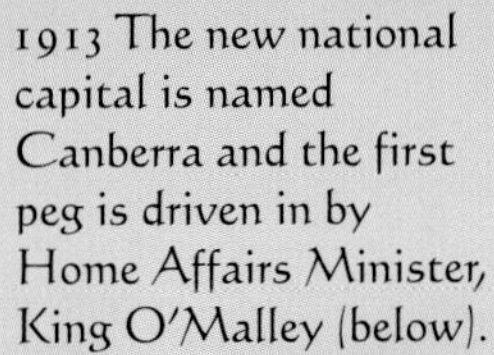

1913 The new national capital is named Canberra and the first peg is driven in by Home Affairs Minister, King O'Malley (below).

1914 Australia becomes involved in World War I when Britain declares war on Germany.

1915 The Commonwealth introduces its own income tax as a temporary measure to pay for the war.

ANZAC forces land at Anzac Cove, Gallipoli.

1916 ANZAC Day is first celebrated on April 25.

1917 The Commonwealth Police Force is established.

1918 Australia celebrates as the Armistice of 11 November ends World War I. Of the 329 000 Australians who served overseas, 166 819 were wounded and 59 342 lost their lives.

1919 There are many strikes throughout the country. During the year 6 308 226 working days are lost because of strikes.

1920 The Communist Party of Australia and the Federal Country Party are both formed.

LEISURE AND LIFESTYLE

1911 G. Hardwick wins gold medals for Australia in boxing and swimming at the Festival of Empire, the first of the sporting competitions now known as the Commonwealth Games.

1912 Walter Burleigh Griffin (right) wins the international competition for the design of Canberra, Australia's capital city.

1913 A documentary film entitled Home of the Blizzard is released by Frank Hurley, Douglas Mawson's official photographer for the Australasian Antarctic Expedition.

1914 The tango dance from Argentina becomes popular in Melbourne and Sydney.

1915 Visiting Hawaiian, Duke Kahanamoku, introduces surfboard riding to Australia.

1916 Roy Rene, 'Mo', first appears at the Princess Theatre in Sydney.

1917 The Australian boxer, Les Darcy (above), dies in Memphis, Tennessee, from pneumonia.

1918 The children's classics, Snugglepot and Cuddlepie by May Gibbs, and The Magic Pudding by Norman Lindsay (left), are published.

1919 The film, The Sentimental Bloke, produced by Raymond Longford, opens in Melbourne.

1920 Raymond Longford releases the first film version of Steele Rudd's Dad and Dave stories, On Our Selection.

The March of Time: **1921 to 1930**

1921–22	1923–24	1925–26	1927–28	1929–30

EVENTS

1921 The Ford Motor Co. begins assembling cars in Australia.

1922 The Smith Family Welfare Organisation and the Country Women's Association are both established.

1923 Fred Walker and Co. begins producing Vegemite.

1924 The longest recorded heatwave in Australia ends. The temperature at Marble Bar, Western Australia, had exceeded 100° F (38° C) for more than 170 consecutive days.

1925 Radio 2UE begins operating. It is to become Australia's oldest commercial radio station.

1926 The prickly pear infestation is successfully eradicated by the release of eggs from a South American moth.

1927 The Flying Doctor Service is established by the Reverend John Flynn.

1928 Bert Hinkler makes the first solo flight from England to Australia and Charles Kingsford Smith (left) and Charles Ulm make the first trans-Pacific flight from California to Brisbane.

1929 Noel Hunt introduces air-conditioning into Australia.

1930 The first commercial radio telephone service is established between Australia and England.

GOVERNMENT AND FOREIGN AFFAIRS

1921 Prominent social worker and Nationalist, Edith Cowan, becomes the first female member of any Australian Parliament when she is elected to the Western Australian Legislative Assembly.

1922 Payment for six days sick leave per year is introduced by the Commonwealth Arbitration Court.

1923 Queensland's Labor government introduces Australia's first unemployment benefits scheme.

1924 About two million koala skins are exported this year resulting in near extinction of koalas in the eastern states.

1925 Working hours are reduced to forty-four hours per week in NSW and Queensland.

1926 The Council for Scientific and Industrial Research (later CSIRO) is established.

1927 (Above and left) Parliament House, Canberra, is officially opened by the Duke of York.

1928 A Court of Enquiry justifies the killing of thirty-two Aborigines by whites in retaliation for an Aboriginal attack on a station holder and the killing of a white dingo shooter.

1929 The Scullin Labor government abolishes compulsory military training and voluntary enlistment is introduced.

1930 Unemployment of workers reaches 20% as Australia experiences the effects of the worldwide Depression.

LEISURE AND LIFESTYLE

1921 W. B. McInnes wins the first Archibald Prize for his portrait of Mr H. Desbrowe-Annear.

1922 'Along the Road to Gundagai', written by Melbourne songwriter Jack O'Hagan, is published in sheet music.

1923 The English novelist, D. H. Lawrence, writes his novel, Kangaroo, while living at Thirroul, NSW.

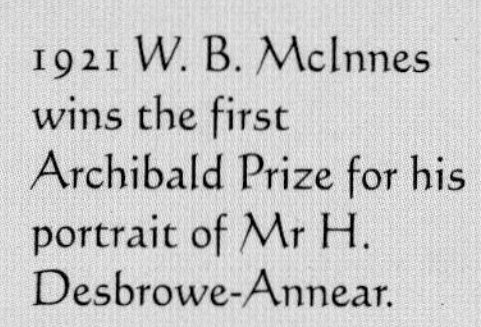

1924 Three Australians win gold medals at the Paris Olympics: A. W. Winter for the hop, step and jump, R. C. Eve for diving and Andrew 'Boy' Charlton (left) for the 1500 metres freestyle (sets record).

1925 The first professional jazz record is made featuring the trombone and trumpet playing of Frank Coughlan.

1926 The Russian ballerina, Anna Pavlova, tours Australia promoting public interest in ballet. Robert Helpmann studies with her company during the tour.

1927 Australia's first greyhound races are held at Harold Park, Sydney.

1928 The first 'talkies' films are screened for the Australian public in Sydney: The Jazz Singer at the Lyceum and The Red Dance at the Regent Theatre.

1929 (Above) Doris Fitton establishes the Independent Theatre in Sydney.

1930 Phar Lap (left) wins his second Melbourne Cup.

The March of Time: **1931 to1940**

1931–32	1933–34	1935–36	1937–38	1939–40

EVENTS

1931 Western Australia's largest nugget, the Golden Eagle, weighing 35 303 grams, is found at Coolgardie.

1932 The Sydney Harbour Bridge is officially opened by Premier Jack Lang (right).

1933 The Australian Women's Weekly begins publication.

1934 'Cook's Cottage' arrives from England and is reassembled in Fitzroy Gardens, Melbourne.

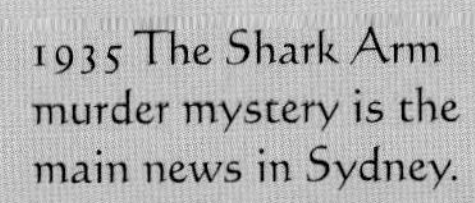

1935 The Shark Arm murder mystery is the main news in Sydney.

Kingsford Smith and Tom Pethybridge are lost over the Bay of Bengal in the Lady Southern Cross.

1936 The Hume Dam on the Murray River is completed. It is Australia's largest public works to this time.

1937 A serious epidemic of infantile paralysis (poliomyelitis) breaks out in all states.

The Spirit of Progress begins its first run from Melbourne to Albury.

1938 Australia's first Empire Games (now the Commonwealth Games) are held in Sydney as part of Australia's 150th Anniversary.

1939 Devastating bushfires in Victoria, NSW and Tasmania destroy millions of hectares of forest and claim seventy-one lives.

1940 Dr Howard Florey and Dr E. Chain successfully prove the antibiotic qualities of penicillin. They are awarded the Nobel Prize in 1945. Florey is the first Australian to receive this award.

GOVERNMENT AND FOREIGN AFFAIRS

1931 The Commonwealth Arbitration Court reduces the basic wage by 10% to try to combat the worsening depression.

1932 Dole queues lengthen and unemployment peaks at 30% as Australia becomes seriously affected by the Depression.

1933 Australia takes control of six million square kilometres of the Antarctic continent when the Australian Antarctic Territory is created.

1934 A dictation test is used to bar a Czech Communist, Egon Kisch, from entering Australia to address an anti-war congress.

1935 Mild trade sanctions are imposed against Italy after it invaded Ethiopia, and HMAS Sydney is sent to join the international force at Gibraltar.

1936 The Federal Arbitration Court grants a week's paid annual leave to commercial printers.

1937 A Federal government conference adopts a policy of assimilation for part-Aborigines and establishes reserves for the segregation of full-blood Aborigines.

1938 Australia agrees to accept Jewish refugees from Nazi Germany.

1939 Prime Minister, Robert Menzies, announces Australia is at war with Germany.

1940 The government bans the Communist and Fascist political parties in Australia believing them to be subversive to the war effort.

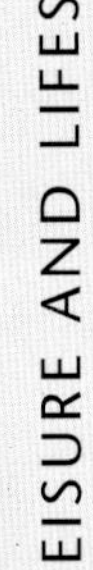

1931 The first fully Australian newsreel, Cinesound Review, has its first showing.

1932 West Australian Walter Lindrum becomes the world billiard champion.

1933 The 'bodyline' bowling controversy begins with the Australia v England Test cricket series.

1934 Science House in Gloucester Street, Sydney, is the first winner of the John Sulman Award for Architecture.

1935 The ABC begins school radio broadcasts.

1936 The 'Dad and Dave' (below) radio serial begins. It will be broadcast for fifteen years.

1937 The Police Citizens Boys' Club movement is opened in Sydney to help in the fight against juvenile delinquency.

1938 Albert Namatjira, (below) an Aboriginal artist, holds his first exhibition in Melbourne, selling all forty-one paintings.

1939 Edouard Borovansky opens a ballet school in Melbourne which eventually becomes the Australian Ballet.

1940 George Russell Drysdale begins his landscape paintings of the Australian outback.

The March of Time: **1941 to 1950**

1941–42	1943–44	1945–46	1947–48	1949–50

EVENTS

1941 Dr Norman Gregg establishes the connection between rubella (German measles) and congenital defects in babies.

1942 Darwin is bombed by Japanese aircraft and three midget submarines enter Sydney Harbour and sink HMAS Kuttabul.

1943 Japanese torpedo the hospital ship Centaur off the south Queensland coast with the loss of 268 lives.

1944 Japanese prisoners-of-war attempt to escape from their POW camp at Cowra, NSW. Four Australian guards die and 234 Japanese are killed or commit suicide.

1945 War with Germany concludes on 8 May and Japan surrenders 15 August.

1946 The government-owned Trans-Australian Airlines is established.

1947 The Australian National Antarctic Research Expedition sets up a permanent scientific research station on Heard Island, Antarctica.

1948 The Holden, an entirely Australian-made car, is produced at General Motors-Holden.

1949 Prime Minister Chifley officially opens the Snowy Mountains Hydro-Electric Scheme for irrigation and power generation.

1950 The CSIRO successfully introduces the myxomatosis virus to the Murray Valley to control the rabbit population.

GOVERNMENT AND FOREIGN AFFAIRS

1941 Australians of the 6th Division capture Tobruk—including 40 000 Italian soldiers— a great morale booster for the people at home.

Following the attack on Pearl Harbour Australia declares war on Japan.

1942 To conserve fuel and electricity daylight saving begins. Petrol, tea, butter, sugar and clothing are rationed and a uniform Federal income tax replaces state taxes.

1943 The first two women elected to Federal Parliament are Dame Enid Lyons (above left) and Dorothy Tangney.

1944 The Commonwealth government extends social welfare and introduces unemployment and sickness benefits.

1945 500 000 people are out of work due to strikes over wage claims, the forty-hour week and company policies.

1946 The Immigration Advisory Committee suggests mass immigration from Britain and Europe to increase Australia's population. A. Calwell (above) is first Immigration Minister.

1947 The Northern Territory moves towards self-government when it is granted a partly elected and partly nominated Legislative Assembly.

1948 The forty-hour week becomes effective on 1 January throughout Australia.

1949 The Australian Security Intelligence Organisation (ASIO) is established.

1950 The Minister for External Affairs, Sir Percy Spender, proposes the establishment of the Colombo Plan, an aid program for less developed nations. Australian volunteer troops are committed to United Nations forces in Korea (left).

LEISURE AND LIFESTYLE

1941 The Timeless Land by Eleanor Dark (above) and Ernestine Hill's novel My Love Must Wait are published.

1942 The Pea Pickers, a novel by Eve Langley, is published.

1943 There is much controversy when the Archibald Prize is won by William Dobell for his portrait of Joshua Smith.

1944 Charles Chauvel's film Rats of Tobruk is released and Kenneth Slessor publishes One Hundred Poems, 1919–39.

1945 The first Sydney–Hobart yacht race begins on Boxing Day with nine competitors.

1946 Two poets publish their first books of poetry: Judith Wright with The Moving Image and James McAuley with Under Aldebaran.
At the movies, Chips Rafferty stars in the Australian film The Overlanders.

1947 Sydney Nolan exhibits his first Ned Kelly series of paintings.

1948 After twenty years of Test cricket, Donald Bradman retires with a record of 117 centuries.

1949 'Blue Hills', the popular ABC radio serial, commences. It runs for the next twenty-seven years.

1950 Frank Hardy (below) publishes Power Without Glory and Nevil Shute publishes A Town Like Alice.

The March of Time: **1951 to 1960**

1951–52	1953–54	1955–56	1957–58	1959–60

EVENTS

1951 Extensive bushfires throughout all states in Australia claim sixteen lives.

1952 There are heavy rural losses as one of the worst recorded floods in Australian history strikes southern NSW.

Jubilee celebrations are held throughout Australia to mark the fifty years since Federation.

1953 The Atomic Energy Commission is created to co-ordinate the research and development of atomic energy and uranium which has been discovered in Australia.

1954 Queen Elizabeth II and Prince Philip tour Australia, the first visit by a reigning monarch.

1955 The first hydroelectric power for the Snowy Mountains Authority is generated by the Guthega Power Station.

1956 The CSIRO manufactures the Salk vaccine for polio and governments begin a free mass vaccination program.

1957 Danish architect Joern Utzon wins the international competition to design the opera house for Sydney and the Sydney Opera House Lottery begins.

1958 Qantas begins its first commercial around-the-world air service travelling between Sydney and London, with one route via the US, the other via India and the Middle East.

1959 Qantas takes delivery of its first jet aeroplane, an American-made Boeing 707.

1960 Eight-year-old Graeme Thorne is kidnapped and murdered, the first case in Australia of child kidnap for ransom. His parents had won the Opera House Lottery.

GOVERNMENT AND FOREIGN AFFAIRS

1951 ANZUS, Australia's first defence treaty with a foreign country, is signed by Australia, New Zealand and the United States.

1952 Assisted immigration is reduced because of rising unemployment among Australian workers.

1953 The Commonwealth Medical Benefits Scheme is introduced paying pharmaceutical, medical and hospital benefits to members of registered health funds.

1954 Australia becomes a member of the South-East Asia Treaty Organisation (SEATO), the main aim being to prevent communist expansion in South-East Asia.

1955 Australia receives its one millionth post-World War II migrant, Mrs Barbara Porritt from Yorkshire, England.

1956 Britain begins its first testing of atomic weapons on the Australian mainland at Maralinga, South Australia.

1957 The Australia–Japan Trade Agreement provides better access to each country's products.

With no need for a large peacetime army the numbers of National Service trainees are reduced with the introduction of a ballot system based on birth date.

1958 NSW is the first state to introduce equal pay for women doing equal work. Female state school teachers are the first to benefit.

1959 Australia restores diplomatic relations with Egypt (broken off during the Suez crisis) and the USSR (broken off over the Petrov affair).

1960 Social security benefits such as pensions and child endowment are now being paid to Aborigines.

LEISURE AND LIFESTYLE

1951 'The School of the Air' begins broadcasting to children in remote areas from the Flying Doctor Service in Alice Springs.

1952 Australia's first world boxing title is won by bantamweight Jimmy Carruthers (below).

1953 The exhibition, 'French Painting Today', begins a nine-month tour of Australia, encouraging abstract impressionism.

1954 The Elizabethan Theatre Trust is formed to encourage the development of drama, opera and ballet.

1955 Barry Humphries' Edna Everage impersonation first appears during a Christmas review in Melbourne.

1956 Television commences transmission in Australia in time to broadcast the Melbourne Olympics, the first time the Olympics have been broadcast on TV.

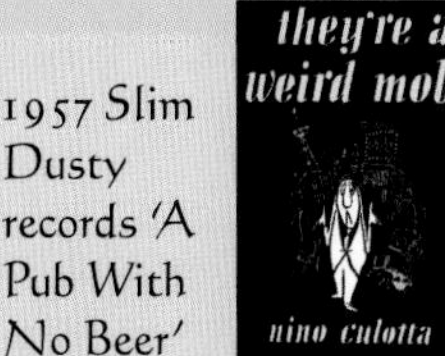

1957 Slim Dusty records 'A Pub With No Beer' and it becomes Australia's first gold record.

Small Sydney firm Ure Smith publish Nino Culotta's (John O'Grady) They're a Weird Mob which sets a sales record unbeaten until the 1980s.

1958 Sydney's Radio 2UE presents Australia's first Top 40 chart and Brian Henderson's program 'Bandstand' begins on TV.

1959 The musical My Fair Lady opens in Melbourne and runs for five years. The ABC's '6 O'Clock Rock' begins on TV, compered by Johnny O'Keefe, Australia's 'King of Rock'.

1960 The largest exhibition of Australian Aboriginal art yet seen tours Australia.

During the fifties women's fashions had been chic, with a well groomed look.

The March of Time: **1961 to 1970**

1961–62	1963–64	1965–66	1967–68	1969–70

EVENTS

1961 Large-scale iron-ore deposits are found in Western Australia and the first commercially viable oilfield is discovered in Queensland.

1962 The Southern Aurora begins through-services by train between Sydney and Melbourne following the extension of the standard gauge from Albury to Melbourne.

1963 The Bogle–Chandler inquest begins. Their bodies had been found in Sydney bushland, the cause of death remaining a mystery.

1964 HMAS Voyager sinks with the loss of eighty-two lives after colliding with HMAS Melbourne (above) during naval exercises off the coast of NSW.

1965 English model, Jean Shrimpton, wears an above-the-knee dress, no hat and no stockings to Flemington. She is asked to dress more conventionally for the Melbourne Cup.

1966 Decimal currency is introduced.

1967 Australia's first satellite is launched from Woomera, and a national four-digit postcode system is introduced to assist in the sorting of mail.

1968 Australia's first heart transplant operation takes place in Sydney. The patient survives for forty-five days.

1969 Television pictures of man's first landing on the moon are relayed to the world from the CSIRO's radio astronomy telescope near Parkes, NSW.

Great UK train robber Ronald Biggs (right) is reported living in Melbourne.

1970 The Royal Family and Pope Paul VI (the first pope to visit Australia) help celebrate the 200th anniversary of Captain Cook's landing.

GOVERNMENT AND FOREIGN AFFAIRS

1961 Unemployment reaches 3.5% during the Menzies government 'credit squeeze' which particularly affects the motor vehicle, building, timber and steel industries.

1962 Aborigines in Western Australia, Queensland and the Northern Territory gain the right to vote in Federal elections; the same right that Aborigines in other states have had since 1949.

1963 Australia signs the Nuclear Test Ban Agreement.

1964 Financial assistance is given to government and non-government secondary schools for science education, thus re-introducing state aid to private schools after a lapse of over 100 years.

1965 Australia sends troops to Vietnam, a decision which is bitterly opposed by the Labor Party, and the first National Service call-up ballot is held.

1966 As a result of a strike on Wave Hill Station (Northern Territory) the Northern Territory Aboriginal stockmen are granted white rates of pay and working conditions and the Council for Aboriginal Rights is established.

1967 A record 'yes' vote in the referendum grants Aborigines full citizenship rights giving the Federal government power to legislate for Aboriginal policy and include them in the census.

Prime Minister Harold Holt drowns in the surf at Cheviot Beach, Victoria.

1968 The 12-mile fishing limit around Australia is introduced to protect the Australian fishing industry. John Gorton (left) succeeds Harold Holt as Prime Minister.

1969 The Conciliation and Arbitration Commission grants equal pay to women for equal work.

1970 Tempers flare when thousands march in Vietnam War Moratoriums in all states to protest against Australia's participation in the Vietnam War.

LEISURE AND LIFESTYLE

1961 Government-run Totalizator Agency Boards (TABs) have been introduced to take over control of off-course betting in Victoria and Western Australia.

1962 Firsts in tennis—Rod Laver wins the Grand Slam (Australian, French, Wimbledon and US singles titles) while Margaret Smith wins the US, Australian and French singles titles.

1963 The Reverend Alan Walker of the Central Methodist Mission in Sydney establishes Lifeline, Australia's first telephone counselling service.

1964 The Beatles tour Australia and 'Beatlemania' spreads.

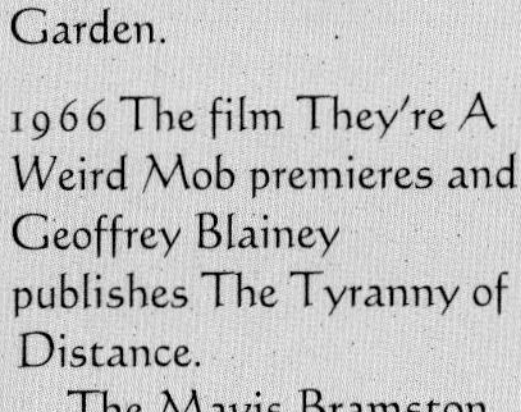

1965 The Seekers' song 'I'll Never Find Another You' becomes the first Australian record to sell a million copies.

Joan Sutherland returns home for an Australian opera tour and the Australian Ballet makes its first overseas appearance at Covent Garden.

1966 The film They're A Weird Mob premieres and Geoffrey Blainey publishes The Tyranny of Distance.

The Mavis Bramston Show (left) begins on the Seven Network.

1967 The ABC's current affairs program, 'This Day Tonight', is launched with Bill Peach as compere.

1968 The Australian Council for the Arts and the National Literature Board of Review are established.

1969 Harry M. Miller presents the live rock-musical Hair at the Sydney Metro.

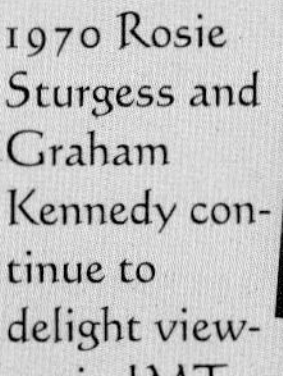

1970 Rosie Sturgess and Graham Kennedy continue to delight viewers in IMT on the Nine Network.

The Women's Liberation Movement is greatly influenced by the publication of Germaine Greer's (left) The Female Eunuch.

The March of Time: **1971 to 1980**

1971–72	1973–74	1975–76	1977–78	1979–80

EVENTS

1971 The South African Springbok Rugby Tour sparks anti-apartheid demonstrations wherever the team plays. A State of Emergency is declared in Queensland.

1972 The Ord River Dam, part of the Ord River Scheme in the Kimberleys, Western Australia, is officially opened.

1973 The Sydney Opera House is officially opened by Queen Elizabeth II and the Wrest Point Casino, the first legal casino in Australia, is opened in Hobart.

1974 There is severe flooding in Brisbane caused by Cyclone Wanda and on Christmas Day Darwin is devastated by Cyclone Tracy.

1975 The bulk carrier, Lake Illawarra, sinks, losing twelve lives, when it rams and destroys a span on the Tasman Bridge, Hobart, and a fire claims fifteen lives when it destroys the Savoy Hotel in Sydney.

1976 The ACTU calls the nation's first general strike to protest against proposed changes by the Fraser government to Medibank.

1977 Eighty-three lives are lost in Australia's worst rail disaster, at Granville in Sydney.

1978 Refugee 'boat people' (right) arrive in Darwin from Vietnam, Laos and Cambodia.

1979 The British government takes responsibility for the disposal of plutonium waste excavated from the Maralinga bomb test site in South Australia.

1980 An anti-venene for the funnel-web spider bite is discovered by CSIRO scientists.

GOVERNMENT AND FOREIGN AFFAIRS

1971 Queensland's Neville Bonner becomes the first Aboriginal parliamentarian.

1972 Gough Whitlam becomes the first Labor Prime Minister since 1949. His government ends conscription and recalls the remaining Australian troops from Vietnam.

1973 The Federal government grants Papua New Guinea self-government (comes into effect in 1975), gives eighteen-year-olds the right to vote in Federal elections, abolishes tertiary education fees and appoints Elizabeth Reid adviser to the government on women's affairs (first in the world).

1974 The Bankcard credit system is introduced by government and private banks.

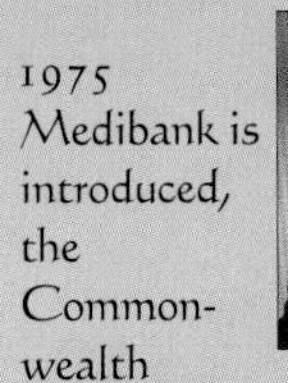

1975 Medibank is introduced, the Commonwealth Racial Discrimination Act becomes effective and the Whitlam government is controversially dismissed by the Governor-General, Sir John Kerr (above).

1976 The Family Court of Australia introduces 'no-fault' divorce based on twelve months' separation as proof of irretrievable breakdown.

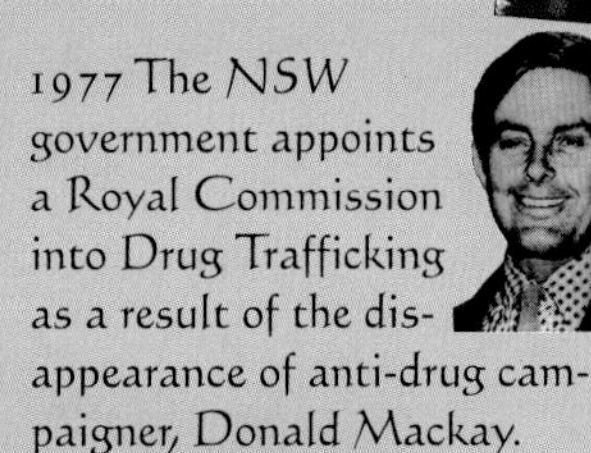

1977 The NSW government appoints a Royal Commission into Drug Trafficking as a result of the disappearance of anti-drug campaigner, Donald Mackay.

1978 Three die as a terrorist bomb explodes outside the Sydney Hilton Hotel where the Commonwealth Heads of Government Meeting is being held. A State of Emergency is declared.

1979 Up to twelve months unpaid maternity leave is granted to working women by the Commonwealth Arbitration Commission.

1980 After much controversy, the Tasmanian government decides to dam the Gordon River as part of a hydro-electricity scheme, at a place least damaging to the environment, and the Franklin River and its surroundings becomes a national park.

LEISURE AND LIFESTYLE

1971 The NSW Builders Labourers Federation imposes 'green bans' on the Rocks area in Sydney.

1972 Shane Gould, aged fifteen, is Australia's outstanding performer at the Olympic Games when she becomes the first to hold all women's freestyle swimming records at once.

1973 Patrick White becomes the first Australian to win the Nobel Prize for Literature and the National Australian Gallery purchases Jackson Pollock's Blue Poles.

1974 'Advance Australia Fair' becomes the new national anthem.

Women's fashions favour wide flairs and high platform soles.

1975 Peter Weir's film Picnic At Hanging Rock premieres and colour TV is officially introduced.

1976 The Australian films Caddie, The Devil's Playground and Don's Party are released.

1977 Methodist, Congregational and some Presbyterian churches join to form the Uniting Church of Australia.

1978 A female, Pat O'Shane, becomes the first Aboriginal law graduate and barrister.

1979 Karen Pini and Mike Walsh launch the first Lotto draw in New South Wales. The Federal government introduces the 'Life Be In It' campaign.

1980 Candice Reed, Australia's first 'test tube' baby, is born in Melbourne.

Alan Bond makes a challenge for the America's Cup with his yacht Australia (left).

The March of Time: **1981 to 1995**

1981–1995

EVENTS

1981 Kakadu National Park, the Willandra Lakes and the Great Barrier Reef are given world heritage listing.

1982 The first shipment of uranium ore leaves for processing in America.

1983 The 'Ash Wednesday' bushfires destroy large areas of rich grazing country in Victoria and South Australia; seventy-one people die and seven townships are destroyed.

1984 The Federal government appoints a National Advisory Committee on problems associated with AIDS.

1985 Australia's first communications satellite, Aussat I, is successfully deployed from the space shuttle Discovery.

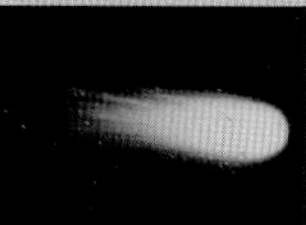

1986 Halley's Comet reappears in Australian skies but is barely visible to the naked eye.

1987 Dick Smith becomes the first person to reach the North Pole by solo helicopter.

1988 On Australia Day, about two million people watch the First Fleet Re-enactment as Australia begins celebrating 200 years of white settlement.

1989 The most severe earthquake in

Australia's history devastates Newcastle, NSW.

1990 Catastrophic floods destroy townships in Queensland, NSW and Western Australia.

1991 Sydney is shocked and saddened when heart transplant specialist, Dr. Victor Chang, is shot dead in a Mosman street.

1992 Inventors and engineers, headed by Doug Tarca, develop a portable oil containment system so that ships can contain their own oil spills immediately.

1993 Compass Airlines goes into liquidation.

1994 The worst bush fires in NSW's documented history destroy bushland and property and claim four lives.

A lodge at Thredbo, NSW is destroyed in a mudslide. Australia mourns the loss of 12 lives. An enquiry subsequently finds that water leaking from underground pipes contributed to the disaster.

GOVERNMENT AND FOREIGN AFFAIRS

1981 Australia's immigration policy emphasises family reunion and filling gaps in the labour market.

1982 Australian troops join United Nations Peacekeeping Forces in the Sinai during Israel's withdrawal from Egyptian territory.

1983 The Labor Party, led by Bob Hawke, wins the Federal election as unemployment reaches 10.7%, the highest level since the Depression years.

1984 Medicare is introduced, financed by a 1% levy on taxpayer's wages.

1985 The Mutitjulu people become the official owners of an area of national park which encompasses Uluru and Mount Olga.

1986 The Proclamation Act, which breaks the legal ties between Australia and Britain, is signed by Queen Elizabeth II in Canberra.

1987 The Fitzgerald Inquiry into police and political corruption and organised crime in Queensland opens.

1988 Australia's new Parliament House is opened in Canberra by Queen Elizabeth II.

1989 The Muirhead Royal Commission Report into Aboriginal Deaths in Custody is released and recommends law reform for minor offences.

1990 Australian sailors and ships leave for the Persian Gulf to join the United Nations Gulf blockade after Iraq invades Kuwait.

1991 Paul Keating replaces Bob Hawke as Prime Minister.

1992 The High Court hands down the 'Mabo Judgement' which rejects the doctrine that Australia was terra nullius at the time of British settlement in 1788.

1993 Prime Minister, Paul Keating, campaigns for an Australian republic and a new flag. He is supported by public opinion polls.

1994 NSW MP John Newman is killed in an unprecedented political assassination.

1995 John Howard replaces Alexander Downer as Federal Opposition leader.

Veteran labor politician Fred Daley dies and is remembered with affection by both sides of the house.

LEISURE AND LIFESTYLE

1981 The government-funded Australian Institute of Sport opens in Canberra.

1982 The Commonwealth Games are held in Brisbane, Thomas Keneally wins the

Booker Prize for Schindler's Ark, The Australian National Gallery opens in Canberra and the Australian film Mad Max II is an unprecedented success.

1983 Alan Bond's winged-keeled yacht, Australia II, wins the America's Cup

1984 Many movie theatres and drive-ins close as the video movie industry gains popularity.

1985 The first Australian Formula One Grand Prix is held in Adelaide, South Australia and the last NSW Opera House Lottery is drawn.

1986 Pope John Paul II visits Australia. Catholicism has become the nation's most popular religion.

1987 Kylie Minogue and Jason Donovan are popular stars in the TV show 'Neighbours'.

1988 Brisbane hosts World Expo '88.

1989 The Adelaide Plaza is completed with the opening of Exhibition Hall.

1990 Joan Sutherland gives her farewell performance in the Sydney Opera House before retiring.

1991 Yothu Yindi becomes Australia's first Aboriginal musical group to be internationally recognised.

1992 The film Strictly Ballroom premieres to the best box office attendance of all movies released in Australia this year.

1993 Australians celebrate as Sydney is awarded the Olympic Games for the year 2000.

1994 The films The Adventures of Priscilla, Queen of the Desert and Muriel's Wedding are huge box office successes, with Priscilla winning best costume design at the 1995 Academy Awards.

Meanwhile, guitarist Ike Isaacs, entertainer-actor Maurie Fields and actor John Hargreaves, all well-loved in the community die during the year.

The March of Time: **1996 to 2004**

1996–2004

EVENTS

1996 The world's worst shooting rampage occurs at Port Arthur, Tasmania. 33 visitors to the sight were randomly shot by gunman Martin Bryant, described by a man from his hometown as a 'nice bloke'. He is later gaoled for life.

1998 Prime Minister Howard refuses to say 'sorry' for past governments actions in the treatment of aborigines.

Asian countries go into recession but Australia's economy continues with little change despite dire predictions.

Huge seas and high winds cause havoc and loss of life with Sydney-Hobart competitors in the Tasman Sea. Weather Bureaus and race organisers receive criticism and an inquiry is called to investigate the tragedy thoroughly.

1999 Hailstorms cause huge damage in Sydney's eastern surburbs. Restoration of properties takes nine months.

2000 The Australian dollar begins to devalue against the US with record lows and as the year goes on, a downward trend develops which continues during the year. Two young surfboard riders are taken by sharks in separate incidents in the Great Australian Bight on the South Australian coast.

2001 Ansett Airlines, insurance giant HIH and telephone company One.Tel all collapse over a short period causing personal losses and job losses to thousands.

Australian elite military forces are sent to assist the U.S. in Afghanistan.

2002 Asylum-seekers are held in detention centres throughout the country sparking nationwide protests.

Interest rates begin to rise after years of living in a low interest environment have effectively stimulated the home building and buying markets.

2002 A nightclub in Bali is bombed by agents of Jemah Islamiah killing 88 Australian citizens and wounding many. Australians become aware that terrorism is now close.

2003 An outbreak of SARS in China threatens tourists worldwide. Australian health experts are called in to help prevent the spread of the deadly disease. The tourist industry is severely effected throughout the world.

GOVERNMENT AND FOREIGN AFFAIRS

1996 John Howard is elected Prime Minister in a landslide to the Coalition.

1998 The Coalition is re-elected with a much-reduced majority after going to the polls with a package of tax-reform and a 10% GST.

A Peoples' Convention is held to present a model for an Australian Republic.

1999 The Indonesian militia refuse to accept a vote for separation of East Timor from Indonesia. Australian peacekeeping forces are sent under a UN plan.

The proposed Australian Republic is defeated at a referendum.

2000 Successful Australian troops return from East Timor and are replaced by an international UN unit.

2001 Some Australians perish in the Al Queda attacks on the World Trade Centre in New York and the Pentagon in Washington on 11 September.

The Coalition is re-elected with an increased majority.

2002 Australian troops continue to fight in Afghanistan and naval ships continue to work with the United States Navy in the Persian Gulf.

Australian Democrats become unsettled when former leader Meg Lees' comments on the sale of Telstra are interpreted as being against policy. She resigns from the party and takes her place in the Senate as an Independent.

2003 The Government commits Australian forces to assist British and United States troops to invade Iraq and find alleged weapons of mass destuction. The United Nations does not support the action. Australians are cautiously supportive of the Prime Minister's decision though large numbers are opposed. The war starts on 20 March and on 1 May the United States President declares it over. There are no Australian troop casualties but a number of journalists are killed.

2003 Mark Latham succeeds Simon Crean as Federal Labor Opposition Leader.

2004 Opinion polls indicate growing support for Mark Latham which poses a serious threat to the incumbent Coalition Government. His later stance on bringing troops home from Iraq by Christmas however meets with political and to some extent, popular disapproval.

LEISURE AND LIFESTYLE

1997 Following the huge success of the Australian movie Babe it is announced that a sequal Babe: Pig in the City is also to be made in Australia.

1998 The Super-League-ARL fight is resolved with the formation of the National Rugby League and a revamped competition. There is controversy as old clubs are excluded from the competition or combined with others.

1999 Fox Studios opens at the former Royal Agricultural Society site at Moore Park, Sydney. With a theme park and film production facilities, movie making in Australia blossoms. International film successes such as The Matrix and Mission Impossible II are made at the new studios.

2000 The Olympic Games in Sydney are hugely successful and are hailed by IOC President Juan Antonio Samaranch as the 'best ever'. The Paralympic Games achieve unprecedented public support.

2001 A world record is set when Australian cricketers win 16 consecutive matches. Leyton Hewitt is dubbed the number one player in world tennis but Pat Rafter is defeated by Goran Ivanisevic at Wimbledon. The Wallabies secure all RU trophies including beating the Barbarians for the first time.

2002 Shane Warne is suspended from playing cticket at any level after being found guilty of taking a performance enhancing drug.

Australia continues to dominate in cricket and tennis and does well at the Winter Olympics and the Commonwealth Games in Manchester.

2003 The Australian team defeats Spain to win the Davis Cup once again.

The Rugby World Cup is held in Australia 10 October—22 November. Australia performs well throughout but is beaten by England.

2004 Olympic swimmer and world 400 metre record holder Ian Thorpe accidently makes a false start at Olympic trials and is disqualified from defending his title in Athens.

Rape allegations grow against Australian football and soccer players.

Index

Arufura
Timor Sea
INDIAN OCEAN
Melville Island
Bathurst Island
Darwin
Kakadu National Park
Border Store
Humpty Doo
Rum Jungle
Adelaide River
Pine Creek
ARNHEM LAND
Nitmiluk (Katherine Gorge) National Park
Elsey National Park
Joseph Bonaparte Gulf
Wyndham
Kununurra
Lake Argyle
Victoria River Downs
Daly Waters
Purnululu National Park (Bungle Bungles)
THE KIMBERLEYS
Derby
Geikie Gorge
Halls Creek
Fitzroy Crossing
Broome
Wave Hill
Elliot
Tennant Creek
Brunette Downs
GREAT SANDY DESERT
PINNACLE DESERT
Port Headland
Marble Bar
Dampier
Roebourne
Barrow Island
Wittenoom
Onslow
North West Cape
Exmouth
Cape Range National Park
THE PILBARA
HAMERSLEY RANGE
Tom Price
Karijini National Park
Newman
Mundiwindi
Lake Disappointment
GIBSON DESERT
Winning Pool
Mount Vernon
WESTERN AUSTRALIA
Kennedy Range National Park
Pt. Quobba
Carnarvon
Milgun
Shark Bay
Dirk Hartog Island
Denham
Meekatharra
Wiluna
Cue
Mount Magnet
Sandstone
Leonora
Kalbarri National Park
Kalbarri
Yalgoo
Mullewa
Geraldton
Dongara
Carnamah
Lake Barlee
Lake Moore
Bonnie Rock
Kalgoorlie
Coolgardie
Boulder
Zanthus
Moora
Nambung National Park
Southern Cross
Lake Cowan
Perth
Northam
York
Rottnest Island
Fremantle
Hyden
Norseman
Balladonia
Pinjarra
Lake King
Salmon Gums
Bunbury
Collie
Pingrup
Esperance
Katanning
Hopetoun
Cape Leeuwin-Naturaliste National Park
Augusta
Normalup
Denmark
Albany
King George Sound
GREAT VICTORIA DESERT
NULLARBOR PLAIN
Forrest
Eucla
Nullarbor
Eyre
Great Australian Bight
NORTHERN TERRITORY
Rabbit Flat
The Granites
Devils Marbles
Yuendumu
Glen Helen
MACDONNELL RANGES
Ormiston Gorge
Finke Gorge National Park
Alice Springs
Kings Canyon
Rainbow Valley Cons. Res.
PETERMANN RANGES
Giles
Uluru-Katatjuta National Park
MUSGRAVE RANGES
Marla
SOUTH AUSTRALIA
Coober Pedy
Ooldea
Stuart Creek Opal Di
Penong
Ceduna
Streaky Bay
EYRE PENINSULA
Port Lincoln
Flinders Chase National Park
Kangaroo Is